E is for

Nancy Polette's

Everybody

*A manual for bringing fine picture books
into the hands and hearts of children*

SECOND EDITION

Scarecrow Press • Metuchen, N.J., London • 1982

Art consultant: Patricia Gilman

Library of Congress Cataloging in Publication Data

Polette, Nancy.
    E is for everybody.

    Includes index.
    1. Picture-books for children--Handbooks,
manuals, etc. 2. Picture-books for children--
Bibliography. I. Title.
Z1037.A1P59 1982 [PN1009.A1] 028.5 82-10508
ISBN 0-8108-1579-6

CONTENTS

E IS FOR EVERYBODY!
(photo courtesy of Lindbergh School District, St. Louis County, Mo.)

PREFACE

Many teachers and librarians recognize that method in education often takes precedence over the final result of any learning activity. The 97-percent literacy rate in this country seems to indicate that the methods used to teach reading are highly effective. Yet other evidence indicates that those who have the ability to read often shun the activity unless it is demanded by necessity. For example, a recent Gallup Poll revealed that 83 percent of adults questioned did not read even <u>one</u> book per year!

E IS FOR EVERYBODY is a manual for teachers and librarians who want to start a lifelong love affair with books in every child's heart. It contains details about carefully chosen gems of children's literature in picture-book format appropriate for use in the elementary grades through junior high school. The books summarized and the suggested activities that follow have been selected for their worth as well as for their diversity. The goal of E IS FOR EVERYBODY is to help teachers integrate fine children's books into every part of the curriculum and to reassure both teachers and children that beautiful, meaningful, delightful, and even hilarious rewards await those who are tuned in and not turned off to the reading experience. The author hopes that E IS FOR EVERYBODY will be seen as a valuable tool that should be in the hands of every librarian and teacher who works with children and youth.

WHY READ TO CHILDREN?

Once upon a time the mists of pedagogy thinned and revealed
two castles. They were equipped with the best fluorescent
lighting, sterile washroom facilities, and vast treasure vaults.
Both castles teemed with children. Black-eyed, blue-eyed,
tow-headed, afro-kinked, fat, skinny, knobbly, dimpled, win-
some, belligerent, shy, persuasive, giggly, and trusting.
Each child was a unique and potential genius, having a different character, background, upbringing, and interest level,
with diverse likes and dislikes, tastes and ambitions. In the
treasure vault of each castle was stored and piled at random
an infinite number of boxes. Some were plain, others ornate
with lace trim or tied with strands of gold. There were more
sizes and shapes than there were children, as many textures
and colors as have ever been designed by humanity and by nature.

Both of these castles had custodians. The custodians
had charge of the children and the treasure vaults. One custodian knew what those boxes contained--nourishment for every
kind of hunger. This caretaker had sampled the tasty tidbits,
devoured tough but savory meat, wrestled with bones and sin-
ews. He opened the treasure doors daily to the children, told
them of his lifelong feasts, helped them to open boxes and
sample for themselves, crawled over a precarious pile of
toppling treasures to find a box just the right size for a little pigtailed girl who had been bumped by a falling box and
now distrusted them all. This custodian knew his job to be
pure delight. Feeding the famished children from the infinite
variety of treasure-food, and whetting their appetites for more,
kept him smiling.

The custodian in the other castle kept the door of the
treasure room locked except at specified mealtimes, and even
then he picked out just one perfectly square, undecorated box
for all the children to share. This custodian had not sampled
many for himself. He was timid and too busy parceling out

the contents of the known box to have time to explore further
among the treasures.   Since he distrusted what he had not
experienced, the children, too, felt a reluctance to venture
beyond his one-box offering--that is, except for one small
group of intrepid children who pilfered his key and sneaked
in during the dark of night to sample and delight in their own
stolen and delectable findings.

          This fairy tale could go on and on.   It could tell how
the children flourished who were nourished on a variety of
tempting foods and who learned to explore and uncover new
treasures for themselves daily.   It could show what became
of the starved urchins who rarely sampled the treasure room,
and who were force-fed on neatly stacked workbooks year after
dreary year.   But surely teachers and librarians already recognize themselves as the custodians of the children and treasures.   One hopes that they can foresee for themselves the
joy and warmth generated by the voracious custodian, who has
a lifetime of exciting growth ahead of him WITH the children--
and that they are appalled at the vision of the wizened and
pickled caretaker, whose very lifeblood has turned into rubber
cement.

          The treasures?   Books, of course!   No two alike,
each penned by an author whose experiences in life are unique.
Truly, a child who has been exposed to the unending supply of
ideas and sustenance through contact with books is assured of
continuous, regenerating education.   Great minds of the present and past have left their inspiration for all to sample and
imbibe from the printed page.   How tragic to think that any
child, man, or woman on this earth might not be exposed to
the wisdom, wit, and inspiration of the ages.   And yet it appears to be happening.   Not just in the aboriginal wilds un-
reached by the printed word, but in American classrooms.
Some teachers try and fail.   Others stick to basal readers
and feel that they have done their tenurial duty.   Some encourage just the naturally quick students and concentrate on repeti-
tious skills with slower (but perhaps more imaginative) youngsters.

          Yet it is possible to start a love affair for life with
books in every child's heart.   Let us besiege our students
with books!   Let us love books so much that our very enthusiasm will permeate the class and whet every budding appetite,
no matter how buried under misconceptions it may have been.
If a child has had an unpleasant experience with books, he or
she may permanently catalog all reading as difficult and dis-

tasteful and never discover the pure fun, surprising delight, or touching of hearts that may lurk within those forbidding covers.

What a glorious lot is that of the custodian-teacher: to bring the young and the great together! Books that are worth reading at all (and how many of the great writers of all time have written for, or are read by, children!) are bursting with the passions that concern us all. Love, hate, fear, superstition, remorse, compassion, tenderness, come to life under the pen of an inspired writer. Great works of art bring forth responses in all of us as they touch our religious feeling, our deepest instincts, our determination to have justice and truth. Eternal values lurk within every great and good book, even if it is only the necessity for laughter and delight. One never knows just which book will prick the mental awakening that means true inner growth. One cannot know just which child is ready for a particular concept in a certain book that will burst into his or her mind with a new light and understanding and illuminate all the things that the child has ever known. Hence the necessity for a continuous sharing of a vast variety of types of books, and authors, and subject matters.

★   ★   ★

E IS FOR EVERYBODY can be used as a key to open that great literary treasure vault in any classroom or library. The books included here were not gathered at random from a library shelf but were carefully selected for their worth and for their diversity. Uniformity can be a dangerous commodity. Children have a natural and unquenchable curiosity, which leads them expectantly from one eager pursuit to another. We can take advantage of their diversity of tastes and interests and expose them to the vast numbers of artists who are speaking to them and for them. There is so much to learn, so much to know in this incredible world, and we have the opportunity to turn to artistic specialists who can help to explain the intricacies of life.

Imagination and fantasy are vital ingredients to a full and rich life. They poke fun at reality, play with it, brighten it, and eventually illuminate it. The daily routine of "required" pursuits tends to squelch the creative spirit. The right books can keep it nurtured and alive. The future of humankind may well rest on the creative and imaginative minds that are being nourished in our classrooms. Fantasy need not

be heavy or ponderous.   It is often simmering with chuckles
and surprises.   An assortment of delight and fantasy is included in the book to fertilize and encourage imaginations.

Yet there is no greater magic than that which evolves
from reality and life itself.   In E IS FOR EVERYBODY you
will also find ways to use books that can reawaken or con-
firm the awe and mystery that surrounds all living things.
A sense of wonder and an inherent appreciation of beauty--
whether of a grass blade or a star--are with children.   Books
can help to nourish this to keep alive that reverence for life
and its infinite variety.   Let us be sure that children are
kept in contact with books that can help them to listen more
acutely, look more intently, feel more sensitively, taste more
discerningly, and touch more genuinely the astonishing world
of reality surrounding them.   Let us give our children the
opportunity to be possessed by this spirit of wonder.

Surely one of the greatest needs in the world today is
that of resolving human relations peaceably.   Nations find it
hard to understand one another, as do their inhabitants.   Books
about real people, facing real challenges, having real feelings,
can help children to understand our common problems and
fears.   Books that can evoke an understanding of other peo-

ples, of different racial or cultural backgrounds, are essential in the literary diet. Such books can bless and benefit their readers, and ultimately all others who may be touched by their lives.

How obvious it is, too, that the salt of a little humor enhances any literary meal! Librarians know that children who will not read anything else can often be hooked on a book that is "funny." Thus E IS FOR EVERYBODY is liberally "salted" to entice the most reluctant appetite.

All of us respond to the very sound of language, the flow of words, the variety of tones and combinations of signals: intrigue the ear of babe and philosopher alike. Words are the tools of our thoughts and experience. The creators of many picture books revel in our language, its cadences and intricacies. We can join in their fun of playing with words, in poetry and projects, and help the children's ears to delight in the richness of the English tongue.

★   ★   ★

Teachers ask, "How can I possibly expose children to the tremendous ideas available in books when I can't get them to read the simplest primer with any sense of understanding or meaning?" The quickest and surest method is to read aloud. Read to your class daily, not as an assignment that must be done "for their good," but because you love the book, or the poem, or the paragraph so much that you simply cannot wait until reading period to share it with them. Squeeze reading aloud into every nook and cranny of unused time. Granted, it does require outside time for the teacher to explore and absorb enough books and articles and poetry to find the very things that demand sharing. But the rewards may be startling! When one has established a rapport by sharing exciting things or moving things or funny things with a class of youngsters, a mutual trust builds up that can give an aura of expectancy to any given moment when the teacher reaches for a book. A book can be worth sharing because it means something special to the teacher, because it contains ideas worth discussing, or simply because it promotes some fun activity.

"But why picture books?" a sixth-grade teacher may ask. Because many of them have something of universal value. Because some of the best of them have been missed by many children. Because they are short, easy to fit into stolen moments of the schedule. And because, one hopes, they will entice the reluctant or nonreaders to overcome their inadequacies and the discouragement they may feel by being unable to handle things on their own grade level. If short, easy, fun books can stimulate interesting classroom projects, perhaps the written word will lose its bugaboo to those children who fear and distrust it.

Not all picture books are easy to read by any means. Many were meant by their authors to be read aloud to children, the vocabularies and nuances needing the understanding of an experienced reader. The conventional easy-to-read primary books are necessarily limited in scope by their vocabularies. It is no wonder that some otherwise astute children balk at digesting them for any length of time. And no wonder that inspired artists and writers turn to picture books, where they are not limited by word lists or concepts. Children of today are so bombarded with new and stimulating ideas from media and the pace of life that it is not surprising to find mediocre books lying forgotten in a drizzle on the playground. This is not the likely fate of an inspired picture book loved by a teacher, shared with a classroom, and used as a basis for some unusual activity.

We cannot overlook the fact that many picture books are valuable as artworks alone. Surely children's books are blessed immeasurably today by the number of outstanding artists who are using their talents and time for the young. The variety of media that are used in producing books of dramatic color and exquisite quality is astonishing. Many picture books can be shared simply as a series of artworks, which can lift and mold children's taste for the best. Be sure that your students have time to browse and absorb the form, line, and color that these artists have provided for them. It is possible that one evocative page of beauty will stay with a child forever, as a yardstick upon which he or she unconsciously measures what is worthy against what is trivial.

Every teacher or librarian has heard, when presenting a colorful picture book to older nonreaders, "Oh, that's cinchy! It's a baby book. I don't need a baby book." Children who read effortlessly, and gobble up with joy the words and ideas within the covers of any book, care little whether a book looks hard or easy or illustrated or battered or whatever. Their literary competence has brought security, and the treasures that they have found through the written word have intrigued them into dabbling anywhere and everywhere. But those who are still struggling to get meaning from the squiggles on the page, and whose limp little egos desperately need the sham assurance created by carrying around a "hard" unillustrated, incomprehensible book, need our help.

★   ★   ★

This second edition of E IS FOR EVERYBODY includes reviews of picture books that in the author's opinion are among the best of those published between 1975 and 1982. And, as in the first edition, help is what this book is intended to be.   Help with ideas for promoting worthy and fun books; help in dissolving the stigma too often attached by youngsters to picture books.   Let E IS FOR EVERYBODY be a springboard for your own promotional ideas and a catapult for all future readers simmering in your classrooms.

MARJORIE HAMLIN

HOW TO USE THIS BOOK

The 126 children's books included in this manual cover a broad range of topics, concepts, and ideas. Most books are short enough to be shared within one storyhour time or class period. The description of each book is followed by one or more suggested student activities, which range from dramatizations and media production to art projects, creative writing, and games. Many of the activities are appropriate for use at any elementary grade level. Others are geared specifically for primary, intermediate, or upper grade levels. Some suggested uses of the manual are:

1) Introducing picture books to students of all ages as a regular daily, biweekly, or weekly activity.

   Teachers and librarians are urged to read the summaries of the books, obtain those books that most appeal to them, and use only those titles about which they have genuine enthusiasm. Selecting and using the books and activities through the school year will expose students to a wide variety of ideas, topics, and concepts and steadily build reading appreciation and enjoyment.

2) Correlating picture books and activities with curriculum topics.

   A subject index is provided to assist the teacher or librarian with such correlation.

3) Integrating art activities throughout the year with fine literature for children.

   The techniques suggested in Part Two of the manual are applicable not only to the books described here but to many other favorites as they are shared and enjoyed. Step-by-step directions will help to ensure a successful art/literature experience.

E IS FOR EVERYBODY

Part I

THE BOOKS AND THE ACTIVITIES

1 ★ AARDEMA, Verna. Bringing the Rain to Kapiti Plain.
    Illustrated by Beatriz Vidal. Dial, 1981.

> "This is the great Kapiti Plain.
> All fresh and green from an African rain. "

But one year the rains were very late and a terrible
drought descended, driving out all of the wild creatures.
The beautiful plain grew barren and dry until Ki-pat,
watching his herd of hungry and thirsty cows, spied a
cloud hovering above and came up with an ingenious way
to "green-up the grass, all brown and dead, that needed
the rain from the cloud overhead." Here is a rhythmic
tale meant to be read aloud so that the children can join
in, as they are sure to do!

Activities

1) This short, powerful story should heighten interest in
other books about animal life. The reading of the story
can be followed by a short introduction to (or reminder
of) the location of nonfiction books on animals in the library. A visit to the library can be arranged so that
the librarian can introduce other exciting animal stories
to children. Students should be given time to choose
books they would like to read and a time to share the
books with each other. If available, the Newbery Award
Recordings of Incident at Hawk's Hill will serve as an
enjoyable class listening experience to heighten interest
in factual animal books and stories.

2) An activity for upper-grade students might be a search
of the Readers' Guide to locate magazine articles on
drought and its effect on wildlife. Questions to research

3

might include a) How does drought occur? and b) What
can be done to ease the effects of drought on people?
On animal life?

2 ★ AHLBERG, Janet and Allan.   Funnybones.   Greenwillow,
    1980.

In a dark dark cellar lived a big skeleton, a little
skeleton, and a dog skeleton. One night they decided to
go for a walk and frighten someone, but everyone was in
bed. So the skeletons played in the park, threw sticks
for the dog (with amazing results), sang songs, and
frightened each other until it was time to go home to
their cellar. There's not a shiver in the book but there
are grins and giggles on every page.

Activities

1) This tale is so imaginative it will send children back
several times just to take another peek. Because the
descriptions and illustrations conjure up "spooky" images,
it would be especially effective around Halloween. Let
the children's imaginations run wild in some creative
writing. You provide the setting and then they're on their
own. Your part might go something like this:

During the night you turn into a monster. Your Mother
is calling you to get up and come to breakfast. What
are you going to do? Do you want her to see you like
this? If you don't, what can you do? What made you
turn into a monster? How can you turn this around?

2) Let the children make something that will shiver
naturally--a skeleton. This is made almost entirely from
white strips of paper of varying lengths. Begin with the
head and breastbone, which is one long piece. Glue ribs
inside. Make two bows for shoulders and pelvis. Attach
chains for arms and legs. Cut arms and feet from white
paper. Add facial features with a marker. Hang by
string from the head. A slight breeze will set all bones
shivering.

3 ★ AHLBERG, Janet and Allan. Peek-A-Boo. Viking, 1981.

In this delightful book brief rhyming clues invite chil-

dren to look through actual holes cut in the pages to see
the people and rooms of one home from breakfast to bed-
time. A good exercise in visual perception for the very
youngest and an excellent model for primary children in
making their own Peek-A-Boo pages.

Activities

1) What if your home disappeared? Where would you
look for it? Where might you find it?
    Draw a Peek-A-Boo picture of something in your home.
Below the picture write a clue as to what it is.
    What is a home? Is it different from a house? Can
you have or feel home inside you? What does it feel
like? Could you ever really lose your inside home?
(Talk about the feeling of home, how it includes love and
sharing and unselfishness, qualities that we can take with
us wherever we go. Help the children to remember that
if they ever get lonely they can feel home right inside of
them.)

2) Have children build themselves a home out of odds and
ends, such as bits of scrap paper, light cardboard, paper
straws, bottle caps, etc. Construct it on a piece of 4"
by 6" cardboard.
    Another idea is for each child to choose a letter of the
alphabet and build a home in it. This can be drawn on a
sheet of paper or constructed on a letter cut out of cardboard.
    Take children to a hatchery and bring back some un-
hatched eggs. Devise an incubator and watch the eggs
hatch.

4 ★ ANDERSEN, Hans Christian. The Snow Queen. Adapted
      by Naomi Lewis. Illustrated by Errol LeCain. Viking,
      1979.

      Once upon a time there were two little children who
loved each other very much. But one day Kay, the boy,
was mysteriously taken away by the Snow Queen, touched
as he was by a splinter of glass that turned his heart to
ice. Gerda, the girl, went where the Northern Lights
were burning in search of Kay. After a long journey she
finds Kay and melts his icy heart with a warm teardrop,
releasing him from the castle of the Snow Queen. Told
in rich language and magnificent illustrations, this is an
outstanding book.

Activities

1) Discuss: What is friendship? What things do friends share with one another?
Do you think it is necessary to have a lot of material things in order to enjoy life? Do you think you could find enjoyment in ordinary things if you explored them?
What is meant by the proverb "Birds of a feather flock together"?
Have you ever been lost? Have you ever gone on a trip all alone? How did it make you feel? Would you rather have shared your experiences with a friend at the time?
Do you think animals can show friendship? What behaviors might be associated with friendship?
Why do you think some people seem to see the world through an imp glass?

2) Make a collection of flowers, using either real flowers or pictures, and label them. Then choose a flower and write the story that it might tell.
Learn to make flowers out of tissue paper. Use these for flower arranging, gifts, and decorations.
Plan a trip to your city's botanical gardens for the aesthetics of it.

3) Make January snow month in your classroom. Make scenes from the story as a mural or table display. Construct miniature ski trails, snow-covered mountains, Arctic animals and snow sculptures (made out of Ivory Snowflakes), and reproductions of Kay, Gerda, the Snow Queen, etc. Films on skiing, sledding, and snowball fun can be produced and shown by your fellow classmates. Sound effects can be produced of ice cracking, the swoosh of the skiier, the sleigh bells, the Snow Queen dialogue. A light show could be produced in conjunction with slides of northern countries. A special Sno-Project Activities Area could be set up for research of Sno-facts. An electronic Sno-Quiz game could be developed to test an individual's knowledge of Sno-facts.

5 ★ ANDERSEN, Hans Christian. The Swineherd. Illustrated by Lisbeth Zwerger. Morrow, 1982.

Illustrations of both dramatic and comic quality enhance this new telling of the popular Andersen tale of the foolish

and proud princess who finds life's true values too late.
A poor prince who had only one small kingdom sought the
hand of the daughter of the emperor.   To woo her he
sent as gifts the most beautiful things found in nature, a
rose and a nightingale.   The foolish princess rejected the
gifts and the prince.   Undefeated, the prince dressed as
a swineherd and took a job at the palace, where he finally
discovered how shallow the princess really was.

Activity

Prose to Poetry: There are many ways to create vivid
descriptions of people, places, or things.   Hans Christian
Andersen describes a rose tree in prose.

"There was a rose tree growing on the grave of the
prince's father, and a beautiful rose tree it was.   It
flowered only once in five years, and then it bore only
one rose, but that rose had so sweet a fragrance that
anyone who smelled it forgot all his cares and sorrows. "

With the key words underlined and combined with other
words, a similar description in poetry form reads:

On Father's grave now blooms the tree
A lovely rose for all to see
Only one in five of passing years
The rose did flower to stop all tears.

Challenge students to select another descriptive prose
paragraph in The Swineherd and transform it into poetry.

6 ★ ANNO, Mitsumasa.   Anno's Britain.   Philomel, 1982.

As in Anno's Journey and Anno's Italy, here again is
a rich artistic and intellectual feast with endlessly fas-
cinating details and fresh discoveries at each viewing.
Scenes of famous British landmarks, such as St. Paul's
Cathedral, the Tower of London, Big Ben, Windsor Castle,
and Stonehenge, will be found on close inspection to con-
tain a wealth of historical and literary characters from
Robin Hood to Shakespeare, Isaac Newton to the Beatles,
Sherlock Holmes to Winnie-the-Pooh, Alice in Wonderland,
to the Beatrix Potter characters, and many others.   Such
activities as the Oxford and Cambridge Boat Race, cricket,
fox-hunting, and bagpipe-playing are also included in this

wonderful book, which will provide endless delight to book
lovers of all ages.

Activities

1) Since Anno's books lend themselves so well to discovery after discovery, make a discovery chart for the classroom bulletin board. Headings on the chart can include:
Landmarks, Characters from Literature, Sports, Famous
People, Art. Allow children to fill in the chart as discoveries are made.

2) Students will enjoy, as the culminating activity of a research project on Great Britain, making their own discovery chart of things found in the British Isles. Headings
might include: Animals, Sports, Bodies of Water, Landmarks, Trees, Flowers, Famous People. Compare the
two charts. How complete is Anno's pictorial description
of Great Britain?

7 ★ ARUEGO, José, and DEWEY, Ariane. We Hide, You
       Seek. Greenwillow, 1979.

Rhino plays hide and seek with a variety of camouflage
animals who blend with their natural surroundings. A
sneeze or a clumsy step by Rhino brings the animals into
the open where they can be seen. "Now its my turn to
hide," says Rhino, and chooses the best of all places--a
herd of rhinos exactly like him! An outstanding book to
help children develop perceptual skills.

Activities

1) The concept of camouflage can be introduced after an
oral reading of this book. The chameleon, with its changing protective coloration, is a great place to start. Use
other books on the subject to provide more depth and additional examples. (How Animals Hide, by Robert McClung,
National Geographic Society, 1973, is perfect!) A fun way
to check children's understanding is by allowing each child
to compile a simple scrapbook entitled "Animals Using
Camouflage." Staple three sheets of manila paper between
two sheets of construction paper. Use magazines, especially conservation and nature magazines, to clip and glue
appropriate pictures of camouflaged mammals, reptiles,
and amphibians on the pages of the scrapbook.

2) Rhino's temporary camouflage takes on a silliness,
much to the delight of the children.   Let the children
create their own fun pets.   Provide a large box filled
with magazine pictures of fruits, vegetables, boxes, cans,
utensils, etc., and glue.   Allow each child to select, arrange, and glue his or her own pictures on colored paper.
Display the fun pets and let the silliness permeate the
room.
    Example: A dachshund can be made with a long, yel-
low banana body, two green vegetables for ears, a silver
spoon for a tail that goes up in the air, and four short
cans of tomato sauce for the short legs.

3) This book makes a perfect springboard for writing a
creative story.   Rhino, not being a camouflage animal,
found the only place to hide where he could not be easily
found.   A chameleon, on the other hand, can hide easily
with its ability to change colors so as to blend in with
its surroundings.
    Suppose, after learning about chameleons, the children
wrote their own story about a chameleon that did not know
it could hide by changing colors.   How might the chameleon learn of its ability to change?   Students can be given
sample chameleon patterns to trace around, adding a setting in which their chameleon would be well camouflaged.
Display the stories and drawings with the caption: "Camouflaged Chameleons: Can You Find Mine?"

8 ★ BALIAN, Lorna.   Humbug Rabbit.   Abingdon, 1974.

    The mouse told the Rabbit children that their father
was the Easter Bunny.   Father Rabbit said, "Humbug,"
insisting that there was no Easter Bunny, and that rabbits
do not lay eggs.   Humbug Rabbit is told on two levels.
Above the rabbit burrow, Granny was planning an Easter-
egg hunt for her grandchildren.   Granny couldn't find any
eggs to color because her hen, Gracie, had hidden them.
But Barnaby, the devilish cat, saved the day by showing
Granny where Gracie's hiding place was.   During the night,
after Granny colored and hid the eggs, Barnaby pushed all
the painted eggs down the rabbit hole.   The grandchildren
arrived on Easter morning but couldn't find an egg.   The
Rabbit children discovered the Easter eggs hatching all
over the burrow.   Mother Rabbit shooed her children and
the new baby chicks outside to the delight of Granny and
her grandchildren.   The Rabbit children were so proud of

their father--didn't the mouse tell them he was the Easter
Bunny?

Activities

1) Bring eggs to class and boil them on a hot plate. Have
the children dye them as Easter eggs.

2) Point out that in Humbug Rabbit we were able to see
things that lived above the ground as well as those that
lived below ground. Discuss animal homes and ask the
children to make a chart indicating those animals that
lived above the ground and those that live below. Example:

Homes Above Ground	Homes Below Ground
elephant	rabbit
horse	mole

   Certain animal homes are called by certain terms, for
example, the rabbit's home is called a burrow or warren.
Make up a list of animals and ask the students to go to
the library and find the apporpriate term for each animal's
home.

3) Point out to the students that ecological balance is obtained by animals inhabiting all levels of the environment.
Ask the students to find pictures in old magazines of various animals and place them in the correct level of the
plant environment.

4) For advanced classes: Read Watership Down, by
Richard Adams, orally to the class.

9 ★ BALIAN, Lorna. Leprechauns Never Lie. Abingdon, 1981.

   Lazy Ninny Nanny and Gram lived in a cold, rain-soaked
hut with nothing to eat but rainwater soup.   Instead of
working to thatch the roof, carry water, and dig potatoes,
Ninny Nanny decided to catch a leprechaun and his gold.
Catching the leprechaun was easy but finding the gold
proved a bit more difficult.   In this funny tale the tables
are turned--but to the advantage of Ninny Nanny, Gram,
and the leprechaun!

Leprechauns Never Lie

Activities

1) They say there's a pot of gold at the end of the rainbow and you just have to go after it, or try to get it from a leprechaun who hides the gold. This is really a figure of speech. It is a way of saying that your own wish can come true but you must pursue it.

    Make your own pot of gold. Inside draw a picture of what your pot of gold would be. To make pot of gold:

    a) Enlarge a pattern to desirable size and trace on heavy yellow tagboard or construction paper.
    b) Make a second pot, exactly the same size, out of black construction paper.
    c) Glue black pot on top of yellow pot of gold near pot's rim.
    d) You now have a flap. Lift up black pot and under-

neath, on yellow pot, draw what you wish was
your pot of gold!
e) If you like, decorate the gold like pieces of gold
with crayons, markers, or gold foil.

2) This story adapts easily to a Reader's Theater presentation by adding a narrator to read those lines that
are not dialogue.   No props or costumes are needed,
just readers who can interpret feelings with their voices
--Gram's despair, Ninny's determination and anger, and
the leprechaun's slyness.

10 ★ BALIAN, Lorna.   Sometimes It's Turkey--Sometimes
     It's Feathers.   Abingdon, 1973.

A lovely speckled egg lay in a nest all by itself.
Mrs. Gumm picked it up and hurried home to tell her
friend, the cat.   "A genuine turkey egg.   We'll hatch
it and feed it and let it grow plump.   What a fine
Thanksgiving dinner we will have."   After the wobbly
turkey emerged from the egg and ate everything in sight,
neither Mrs. Gumm nor Cat complained, because Thanksgiving was coming!   The great day arrived with cran-
berry sauce, onion and chestnut dressing, cornbread,
pumpkin pie, and--turkey.   "I have so much to be thank-
ful for," said Mrs. Gumm, "A Thanksgiving feast and
two good friends to share it with."

Activities

1) Using old magazines, ask the children to cut out pictures and make a collage of things that they are "thank-
ful for."

2) Point out to the students the origin of Thanksgiving
Day.   Read them Rodger's The First Thanksgiving or a
similar account.   Ask the children to tell any traditions
their family might observe on Thanksgiving that are similar to those activities of the Pilgrims.   Ask them to
compare their Thanksgiving with Mrs. Gumm's.

3) Many of the foods enjoyed on Thanksgiving and at
other times were here before the first Colonists.   Ask
the children to go to the library and find a list of the
foods we eat that were eaten by the Indians before the
First Thanksgiving.

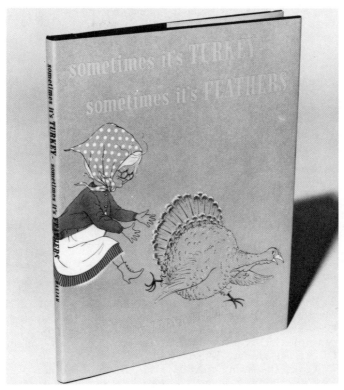

Sometimes It's Turkey--Sometimes It's Feathers

4) Make a Thanksgiving Day cookbook. Collect recipes
from each member of the class. Have each student
write the recipe on a ditto master. Run off enough
pages so that the students can bind all the recipes together into books. The recipes may be for dishes that
their family traditionally serves at Thanksgiving or they
may be for dishes served at the time of the early set-
tlers.

5) Research the production of turkeys by today's farming
techniques. Make a cartoon strip or illustrations in sequence showing each step of the operation.

11 ★ BALIAN, Lorna. The Sweet Touch. Abingdon, 1976.

"Peggy found a penny and
put it into the gum machine,
but instead of a gum ball,
a shiny, genuine plastic
gold ring came out."

When she turned it around on her finger and rubbed
it--to see if the shiny would come off, she conjured up
a genie. But it is only a beginner genie who doesn't
know how to put a stop to the one wish he can grant:
turning everything that Peggy touches into something
sweet.

Activities

1) Read aloud or have the children read the story of
King Midas. Encourage them to identify the parallels
between the characters in The Sweet Touch and King
Midas. There are also parallels in some of the story's
plot. The older children could make a chart showing
how the two stories are similar.

2) The genie in Sweet Touch was named Oliver, The
Magnificent Magic Genie. By using his initials give
Oliver a new name that would indicate his powers. For
example: Oliver the Miniature Muddling Gift-Endower;
Oliver the Minute Messy Guru.
    Using the same initials give Oliver's mother a name.
For example: Olivia, the Mama Ministering to Genies.

12 ★ BALIAN, Lorna.   Where in the World Is Henry? Abing-
       don, 1980.

Henry is missing, and as the question is asked,
"Where in the world is Henry?," the reader is introduced
to the geographic terms indicating the location of Henry.
But after all the terms from street to universe, Henry
is still under the quilt. "Come out of there, Henry!
You know you don't belong on the bed!"

Activities

1) Discuss where the children live. Make an envelope
addressed to each child with his or her entire address
on the front. Example:

John Smith
2617 Pont Avenue
Bridgeton, Missouri 63044
United States of America
North America
Western Hemisphere
Planet Earth
Solar System
Milky Way Galaxy
Universe

2) Using sheets of acetate, ask the students to make
two sets of overlays. One set should include the last
four items from the above address.   The other set
should include the first six items minus the name.
This activity can be adapted to other locations when
studying foreign lands and peoples.

13 ★ BAWDEN, Nina. William Tell. Illustrated by Pascale
      Allamand. Lothrop, Lee & Shepard, 1981.

     Here is a colorfully illustrated new version of an old
tale.   William Tell was a brave hunter who refused to
pay homage to the tyrant Gessler.   For his disobedience
he was forced to shoot an apple from his son's head.
From the dark forest hideaways, stormy seas, and villages of old, here is the tale of a hero and his people
and how Switzerland came to be.

Activities

1) Have children bring current newspapers from home.
Set aside a reading time.   What conflicts do they find
currently in the news?   How can they find more information concerning the reasons for each conflict?
(Readers' Guide, current magazines).   The class can
be divided into two or more groups and a leader chosen
for each.   Members of each group are responsible for
finding reasons for the conflict they research and sug-
gesting solutions to the problem.

2) Primary students might be asked to recall recent conflicts they have had with friends that were resolved peace-
fully.   Children should tell how they resolved their problem or disagreement without resorting to force.

14 ★ BAYLOR, Byrd. If You Are a Hunter of Fossils.
     Illustrated by Peter Parnall. Scribner, 1980.

     Here is a picture book that blends text and illustra-
     tions to show how past and present are found together,
     whether from the waves of the sea that have flowed for
     a hundred million years or from the rocky side of a
     mountain with its fossil secrets revealed for all to see.
     If you are a hunter of fossils--of shells or sponges in
     rocks, or seed fern in shale, or dinosaur tracks or
     bones, you know that every rock holds the memory or
     an earlier time, and young readers will know that they
     will hold it, too.

     Activities

     1) Before reading, ask the librarian to send to the class-
     room a collection of books on endangered species. If
     back issues of Ranger Rick, National Wildlife, and Na-
     tional Geographic are available, these can also be dis-
     played. Allow students ample browsing time with these
     materials. Information gained can be pooled and de-
     veloped into a script for a taped documentary, which
     can become a permanent addition to the school library
     collection for use by other students seeking information
     on the topic.

     2) This is a good book to use to start children thinking
     about the many "gifts" of nature on which we are de-
     pendent and about our responsibility for improving our
     environment. Letters can be written to your state's con-
     servation commission requesting information on the wild
     areas remaining in your state and on good conservation
     practices.

15 ★ BERSON, Harold. Barrels to the Moon. Coward,
     McCann and Geoghegan, 1982.

     The people of Rully liked to sit and look at the moon
     when they weren't working in the vineyards. They en-
     joyed this so much that they thought it would be a good
     idea to unhook the moon and bring it back to Rully,
     where it could be hung on the church steeple and they
     could look at it every day. There was just one problem:
     How would they build a ladder tall enough? Then some-

one remembered the barrels that were used to store the
wine.   If these were stacked one on top of the other,
perhaps they would reach the moon.   Young readers
will enjoy predicting the outcome of the townspeople's
foolish endeavor, particularly, when, being one barrel
short to reach the moon, they decide to remove the
bottom barrel in the stack to place it at the top!

Activities

1) Brainstorm: What tasks were once considered impossible that are now possible?   Examples: staying
under water for a week, and walking on the moon.

2) Brainstorm: What tasks are impossible for humans
to do today?   Which of these do you predict may be
possible in the future?

16 ★ BLEGVAD, Lenore.   The Parrot in the Garret and
      Other Rhymes About Dwellings.   Illustrated by Erik
      Blegvad.   Atheneum, 1982.

"Dormy, dormy dormouse/Sleeps in his little house. /
He won't wake up/Till supper-time, /And that won't be /
Till half-past nine. "   The dormouse who lives in his
snug little house, the old woman who lives in a shoe,
old Mother Shuttle who lives in a coal scuttle, and the
wise old owl who lives in an oak are but a few of the
delightful characters who inhabit even more delightful
dwelling places in this collection of old verse, illustrated
in full color and in black-and-white.

Activities

1) Ask children to fold a sheet of $8\frac{1}{2}$" x 11" white paper
so as to make eight equal-sized squares.   In each square
they are to write a portion of a description of an animal,
including its home.   The eight squares should in total
provide an accurate, illustrated description.   Descriptions should be shared with the class and displayed.

2) Young children need to develop flexibility in their
thinking patterns.   Completing the animal names and
matching each to its home provides a good experience
in flexible thinking.   Examples:

        B__ __R   D__N
        RABB__T   H__ __E

Use many of the combinations found in the book as well:

        D__RM__ __SE LIVES IN HIS H__ __SE
        M__TH__R S__ __TT__ __ LIVES IN A C__ __L
        SC__TT__E

17 ★ BODGER, Joan. Belinda's Ball. Illustrated by Mark
      Thurman. Atheneum, 1981.

      This book is designed to be used with very young
   children. It illustrates early thought processes, especially during the struggle with the concept of object con-
   stancy as defined by Piaget. By participation in the
   story with an adult, a child can discover that a bouncing
   ball is one object, not many; that a lost object may not
   be in the same place it was the last time it was lost;
   and that if it is found in a place that the child cannot
   reach, it may be dislodged with a suitable tool. Oppor-
   tunities are given for the child to be a part of the story-
   telling, which will help in the development of speech patterns. But beyond all this is the fact that the story itself is fun as Belinda loses her ball and then triumphantly
   recovers it.

   Activity

      Object permanence is essential to the development of
   early childhood thinking processes, as it is closely allied
   to the development of conservation (the ability to recognize an object even though it may change form). Without this ability in visual perception the child cannot dis-
   tinguish between large and small letters of the alphabet.
   Set up a "Take Another Look" corner in your classroom.
   Include as many books as you can that require careful
   attention to detail. Many wordless picture books by
   Mercer Mayer or John Goodall will be appropriate, as
   will books by Pat Hutchins and Tana Hoban. The hidden-
   picture page of each issue of Highlights magazine is also
   a valuable addition to such a corner--and, of course, all
   titles by Mitsumasa Anno, who challenges children to look
   again, and again and again! Discussion of the titles is

not necessary: children will let you know of their delight in making many visual discoveries.
     Two additional titles that emphasize the concept of
object permanence are Eat and Be Eaten (Barron's,
1980), by Mari, and Inch by Inch (Obolensky, 1959),
by Leo Lionni.

18 ★ BREITNER, Sue.   The Bookseller's Advice.   Illustrated
        by Jane Chambless-Rigie.   Viking, 1981.

     Simon the Bookseller was often sought after for ad-
vice, for the villagers knew that he was very wise, having
read all of the books in his shop.   What they did not
know was that Simon was hard-of-hearing and often mis-
took one word for another.   The mixups that come about
have happy, if unexpected, results.   Children will enjoy
the humor and see, too, that there is more than one
way to solve a problem!

Activity

     Before sharing The Bookseller's Advice, collect from
the advice column of your local paper several problems
that are appropriate for your grade level.   Divide the
class into small groups.   Give one problem to each
group and let the groups brainstorm for solutions.   After
solutions are shared, let children see if they can match
the columnist's solution with each problem.   They may
discover that more than one solution will work here as
well.

19 ★ CALHOUN, Mary.   Hot-Air Henry.   Illustrated by Erich
        Ingraham.   Morrow, 1981.

     Here is a delightful picture-book flight into fantasy.
It begins when the sassy Siamese cat Henry accidentally
takes off in a hot-air balloon, leaving The Man and The
Kid far below.   As he sails out over the countryside,
Henry enjoys the exhilaration of the dizzying heights,
but he learns that there is more to ballooning than just
watching the clouds go by.   Before the fur-raising flight
is over, he and his balloon are put at the mercy of a
sharp-beaked eagle, blown into a flock of honking, hiss-
ing geese, and led dangerously close to high-power lines.

Here are further adventures of daredevil Henry as he
masters a new sport, a breathtaking journey!

Activities

1) Discuss the following:

    a) What parts of this story could be true and what
       parts are fantasy?
    b) What is exaggeration? What examples of exagger-
       ation do you find in the story?
    c) If you enjoyed Hot-Air Henry, you will also enjoy
       reading or listening to another fantasy classic
       about balloons, The Twenty-one Balloons, by
       William Pêne Du Bois (Viking, 1947). Students
       in grades 3-6 will especially enjoy hearing this
       book read aloud.

2) The class can discuss "exaggeration" as one basic
element of a tale and try making up exaggerated sentences of their own. The fantasy section of the library
should be searched by students for books for individual
reading with time set aside later in the week for a sharing of adventures. Students might enjoy creating their
own life-sized tall-tale character. Ask an especially
tall student to serve as a model for the character by
lying down on a long sheet of mural paper and having
another student trace his or her outline. Cut out the
life-sized "paper doll," on which features, clothing, and
so on will be drawn or painted after the class decides
on what kind of character they will create and what qualities or abilities that character should possess. The
character, of course, should be named and can be
mounted and surrounded by student tales of his or her
exploits.

20 ★ CARLE, Eric. The Grouchy Ladybug. Crowell, 1977.

    At 5 a.m. the grouchy ladybug meets another ladybug
and wants all the aphids on the leaf. After angering the
other ladybug, the grouchy ladybug decides to fight somebody bigger. Each hour the grouchy ladybug meets someone larger than herself (a yellow jacket, beetle, praying
mantis, etc.) until at 5 p.m. she confronts a whale.
The whale is so huge that she can pick a fight with only
one portion of the whale at a time. The whale's tail

slaps the grouchy ladybug so hard that it sends her flying across the sea and she lands right back on the leaf
with the other ladybug. Still friendly, the other ladybug
shares some aphids for dinner with the grouchy ladybug.

Activities

1) The Grouchy Ladybug can fit in well with a science
study of insects. Be certain to go over the characteristics of all insects: three body parts, four wings, two
feelers, and six legs. Since there are so many numbers involved, the children frequently confuse them. A
fun way to check this is to play BUG. Line off a master (see below) and run off copies for the children.
Have the children write the numerals 2, 3, 4, and 6
in the blanks until all boxes are filled. You can make
yourself cards, such as "Cover the number that tells
how many body parts an insect has." These are read
aloud to the children, who then must cover whichever
number they think is correct. When any child has three
boxes in a row covered, he or she calls out BUG!

2) The children might enjoy making an egg-carton ladybug. One carton cup turned upside down will work for
the body. Glue on colored paper for spots and a head
cut from construction paper. Soon the room will be
crawling with friendly ladybugs.

3) Did you know that there are over 280,000 kinds of
beetles in the world? There are more beetles than any
other kind of insect, and insects are the most common

animals in the world! Ladybugs are beetles, so they are members of this enormous clan.

A group activity that will delight middle graders would be the creating of their own "Guinness Book of Beetle World Records: Facts and Fiction." This allows for student research to uncover world-record facts about beetles, such as the fact that one beetle--the African Goliath--is the heaviest insect in the world, weighing over three and one half ounces. The fictitious part of the book would challenge students' imaginations, such as this imaginary fact: the South American mighty winged beetle flies over 75,000 miles a year!

When all students have participated in some way, compile the material in a uniform fashion and bind into a class book.

21 ★ CARRICK, Donald. Harald and the Giant Knight.
       Houghton Mifflin/Clarion, 1982.

Harald always wanted to be one of the Baron's knights. Their bright, clanking armor and brave exploits entranced him. But one spring the knights, without so much as a by-your-leave, took over the land farmed by Harald's family. They trampled the crops and ate the livestock, and the boy began to see his heroes in a new light. In desperation Harald and his parents came up with a plan for getting rid of the invaders. They couldn't be sure it would work, but they plunged into a creation of the biggest and most terrifying knight that anyone had ever seen. Dramatic text and sweeping illustrations.

Activity

Just as Harald and his parents are able to create a terrifying knight, students can create a variety of descriptions of the knight by using slide-a-word sentences.

Words that	huge	Words that	tall
describe	angry	describe	lazily
nouns	mammoth	verbs	majestically

The		Knight stood		against the sky.

22 ★ CHAFFIN, Lillie. We Be Warm Till Springtime Comes.
    Illustrated by Lloyd Bloom. Macmillan, 1980.

    In the bitterly cold house where Jimmy Jack lived
with his mother and baby sister, the wind blew through
the cracks in the walls and wood for the fire was almost
gone. Jimmy Jack remembered an old coal bank on the
hill and set off to try to find fuel. The author's rich,
descriptive language and the haunting illustrations make
this a truly memorable story of a family's love and a
little boy's courage.

Activities

1) Discuss the following:
    Have you ever felt cold? How do you feel when you
come in from playing out in the snow?
    Has your home heating system ever been shut down
for some reason in the wintertime? How did it make
you feel?
    Do you think some poor people suffer during the win-
ter months because of the cost of heating fuel? What
do you think they should do about it? Is there anything
you can do about it?
    Why do you think people sometimes ignore people in
trouble?
    Is there someone who is special to you? Why are
they so dear to you?

2) Visit a museum of science and industry in your city.
Find out about heat. Find out about solar energy. On
returning, prepare drawings or charts in order to share
your knowledge with others.
    Find out more about the energy problem and how it
affects all people, locally, nationally, and internationally.
Invite conservation people into your classroom or write
letters to get the facts. Then plan to do something positive in the way of conservation. Set your goals down in
a visible format, such as a flow chart or bar graph.

23 ★ CHAPMAN, Carol. The Tale of Meshka the Kvetch.
    Illustrated by Arnold Lobel. Dutton, 1980.

    What would happen if all of the things we complain
about turned out to be really as bad as we say they are?
This is exactly what happens to Meshka, the kvetch of

her village. Kvetch means complainer. From morning
to night she could find nothing right. Her son was like
the bump on a kosher pickle; her daughter seemed to
forget that Meshka was alive; her house was a box. And
so it went while the other villagers listened and shook
their heads. Then came the day that Meshka discovered
that things really were as bad as her complaining had
made them seem, and the only cure was almost too difficult for Meshka to achieve.

Activities

1) Cause and effect: Brainstorm: What would cause a
person to complain all the time? Name as many causes
as you can. Brainstorm: What are the effects of being
a complaining person? Name as many effects as you
can.

2) Meshka's complaints finally bring her to the point
where her son IS a pickle, her daughter doesn't know
her, and a large wall pins her to the ground. There
are many ways the author could solve Meshka's problems.
Brainstorm: How many ways could her problem have
been solved other than the solution given in the book?

3) Make a list of all the things you don't like. Make
another list of all the things you do like. Which list is
longer? If your "don't like" list is longer, watch out ...
you may meet the same fate as Meshka.

24 ★ CLEAVER, Elizabeth. Petrouchka. Adapted from Igor
     Stravinsky and Alexandre Benois. Atheneum, 1980.

Here is a lovely illustrated version of the Stravinsky
ballet, in which Petrouchka was a puppet with a soul who
fell in love with a ballerina and tried but failed to win
her. He died, but his spirit lived on in a freedom he
had never known before. The story begins at the fair
with excited children, gingerbread cookies, and a puppet
theater. At the fair Petrouchka was dazzled, but he lost
his life in a fight over the dancer with the Moor. As
the cruel puppet master approached the dead puppet, "a
wild shriek came from the sky. Everyone looked up and
on the roof of the theater they saw the spirit of Petrouchka.
The real Petrouchka was free at last." A beautiful introduction to the world of ballet.

Activities

1) Children, of course, must hear the music after sharing the book. They will delight in identifying parts of the story from the lively fair to the death of Petrouchka. Through discussion, help students to see the universality of music as a communicator.

2) Using some of the puppet patterns found in this book, students can construct the many puppet figures in the story and perform a puppet play of the tale using the ballet music as background for the oral interpretation. Other ballets, as well, are available in picture-book form, including Donna Diamond's Swan Lake (see entry 33).

3) Create your own Dancing Puppet. Play the ballet music from Petrouchka while students do this. The first person in a group or row receives a blank piece of paper. He or she folds the paper in thirds and draws the head of a puppet on the fold at the top of the page. Some lines should extend just into the next fold. The student folds this "beginning" back so that only the extension lines can be seen and passes it on. The next person proceeds in the following fold adding on to what he or she perceives the body to be. This second student folds the picture over and around the first fold so that neither can be seen. Continue in this manner until all folds are completed. Show the finished product. Point out that since everyone added to a picture they couldn't see, with only a few lines to guide them, it is an individual as well as a group product. Students should have some time to discuss what they thought and why. Any criticism is discouraged. If this is new to the students or if enthusiasm is shown, form new groups of three or more and begin again.

25 ★ COHEN, Barbara. Yussel's Prayer: A Yom Kippur Story. Illustrated by Michael J. Deraney. Lothrop, Lee & Shepard, 1981.

Reb Meir and his sons prayed piously all day in the synagogue on Yom Kippur, the holiest of holy days. They waited impatiently for the rabbi to begin the final prayer, a sign that their prayers had entered Heaven and the long day of fasting could end, their sins forgiven.

Yussel's Prayer (illustration © 1981 by Michael J. Deraney)

But the gates of Heaven remained closed until Yussel, tending cows in the nearby pasture, found a way to express his heartfelt prayer to God.   Beautifully told and illustrated.

Activities

1) Discuss: Why do you think Yussel's music opened the gates of Heaven?   Have you ever had an important job?   Can you think of something you do better than anyone else?   Tell (write) us about it.
    If you were asked to do something, and a lot of people depended on you, what are some good qualities that you would want to have   (e.g., resourcefulness, alertness, cheerfulness...)?

2) To discover the importance of working together, games can be played.   Have the children divide into groups. Give each member some unusual object and then have each group, by working together, create and build something (e.g., a special machine, a happy bug...).

Have the class write a poem together with everyone
contributing one line. Pick a theme (wishes, working
together, funny things ...) in order to have some sem-
blance of order in the poem. Let the children call out
their own lines as you write them down. Then read all
of the lines back as one poem.

26 ★ COHEN, Miriam. Jim Meets the Thing. Illustrated by
        Lillian Hoban. Greenwillow, 1981.

Jim was ashamed to be the only one in the first grade
who was scared of the "Thing" on television. But when
a real "Thing" in the form of a praying mantis climbs
on Danny and sends the other first-graders running in
fright, it is Jim who comes to the rescue. Fears can
be very real in young children who have difficulty dis-
tinguishing fact from fantasy. Here is a delightful way
to bring fears into the open, talk about them, and dis-
pel them.

Activities

1) Create a Friendly Creature. To reinforce the idea
that many creatures are imaginary, ask children to
bring to class old magazines from home that can be cut
up. (It is a good idea to do this a day or so before
introducing the book so that the magazines are on hand.)
The class can decide what kind of creatures they want
to create--rare fish, rare bugs, and so on. Children
should look for and cut out a picture of a common object. The picture can be pasted on a plain sheet of
paper and children can add lines and features to create
their own rare creature. The creature should be given
a name. Older children may want to compose a couplet
to describe something their creature does.
    Additional suggestions: If, for example, the class de-
cides to use "rare fish, " a discussion of the characteristics of fish should precede the art activity. Have children especially note how the artist Arnold Lobel has used
the basic characteristics of birds in creating his rare
birds in The Ice Cream Cone Coot (Four Winds, 1971).

2) Ask children to explore the picture-book section of the
library for books about imaginary creatures. Display
the books in a classroom creature-corner for all to enjoy.

The Man Whose Name Was Not Thomas

27 ★ CRAIG, M. Jean.   The Man Whose Name Was Not
      Thomas.   Illustrated by Diane Stanley.   Doubleday,
      1981.

      "Once a good many years ago there was a man whose
name was not Thomas.   His name was not Richard either.
His name was not Bruce or Victor or Henry.   His name
was not Leo or Simon or Charles.   No, his name was
something else!"   So begins a story and guessing game
that tells what does not happen while the pictures show
what does.   A delightful introduction to classification for
young readers and a great patterning model for older
students.

Activities

1) Discuss: Did the hero of this story work or play
the most?
What is work? What is play?
How could we work and get things done and feel the
fun of play too?
Has anyone ever criticized what you like to do? How
did it make you feel?
What is your favorite thing to do or be that most
people haven't discovered yet?
What does this statement mean: "Busy hands are
happy hands"?

2) Let the children draw a picture of the thing that they
like to do most.
Have everyone make posters to decorate and put up
as reminders around the room to KEEP HAPPY.
Some people like to do some things more than others.
Have the children write about such themes as sharing,
getting along, friends are different, and so on.

28 ★ dePAOLA, Tomie. The Clown of God. Harcourt Brace
     Jovanovich, 1978.

Young Giovanni of Sorrento was known throughout Italy
as the marvelous juggler with the clown face, but as the
years passed he and his talent grew feeble and he was
forgotten by those who loved him. Taking refuge in a
church on Christmas Eve, he watched the procession of
the gifts in awe. After everyone had left, he offered
the only gift he had to the image of the Christ Child--
and a stunning miracle occurred.

Activities

1) Ask students to search for pictures of clowns in the
school library. Compare the pictures. Are all of the
clowns happy? Why do some clowns paint sad faces?
If your school is located near a college, invite someone to demonstrate clown makeup.

2) Share The Man on the Flying Trapeze, by Robert
Quackenbush (Lippincott, 1975), the circus life of famed
clown Emmett Kelly Sr., who became a star as Willie,
the lovable hobo clown with the sad face. Suggest that

children might make a mobile with a circus clown in
the center and other performers around him.

29 ★ dePAOLA, Tomie. Fin M'Coul, the Giant of Knockmany
     Hill. Holiday House, 1981.

No giant was more scared of Cucullin, the strongest
giant in Ireland, than Fin M'Coul. Fin escaped Cucullin
many times, but the threat of being flattened by the
giant's thunderbolt remained. One day Fin's wife decided to put an end to Cucullin and prepared a scheme
that is sure to work. When the big giant showed up at
Fin's home on Knockmany Hill, he found that he was in
for a big surprise! Young readers will delight in this
unique solution to a difficult problem.

Activities

1) Small children are particularly fascinated with large
things. In discussing giants, their comments are usually, "If that was me, I would...." Take the children
up on their thoughts and have them recorded on paper.
Suggest that they have just met a giant and became
friends with him (or her). Instruct them to describe
the giant, tell how they became friends, and what things
they do together.

2) Usually, when children draw pictures of themselves
it is on a standard sheet of drawing paper. It would be
fun to have them make a kind of giant picture of them-
selves--at least in proportion to their own bodies. Have
the children pair up so that they can help each other.
Use large craft paper placed on the floor. One child
lays on the paper while the partner draws around him
or her. Then reverse the procedure. After coloring
in all the features (using a mirror to verify details),
the children can cut themselves out. There are a variety of ways to display the giant drawings. The children
might enjoy setting themselves carefully in their own
desks to greet their parents at open house.

3) Use Fin M'Coul as a springboard to a creative-writing
time. Have the students pretend that a scientist has gone
mad and has turned them into giants. Have the children
think about this and try to answer some questions in their
own minds, such as: how did the scientist do this?

What's the mad scientist planning to do with you? What
are you going to do? Then write a good story about
what has happened to you.

30 ★ dePAOLA, Tomie. The Hunter and the Animals. Holi-
     day House, 1981.

    In this turnabout wordless picture book a hunter ap-
pears in the forest, but, being forewarned, the animals
are hidden. Exhausted, he falls asleep and the animals
emerge from hiding, steal his gun and change things in
the forest. When the hunter wakes he cries, thinking
he is lost. The animals then come to his rescue, and,
realizing that the animals are his friends, the hunter
breaks his gun. A book about giving, to be looked at
again and again.

Activities

1) This book can be used to introduce a host of activities appropriate to various age levels. A class nature
walk searching for signs of birds and small animals
might be feasible in some schools.

2) Young student researchers will want to learn more
about homes and habits of creatures of the field, woodland, and meadow. Each child can choose a different
animal or bird for a research project. The school
librarian can be asked to send other books of fiction to
the classroom on small-animal life. Students can select
and read one of the books and tell the story to the class.
Old magazines can be searched for pictures of field or
woodland creatures and the mounted pictures can be given
descriptive student captions.

3) Create a large bare tree in your classroom. It can
be created from cardboard or construction paper and
posted on a wall or a bulletin board. If a nearby woods
is available, locate a dead tree that will fit into the
classroom. Secure it in a bucket of sand so that it is
stable. Have the children help bring the tree back to
life, by adding a green paper leaf each time a child
gives of her- or himself to help another. The giving
can be of time, attention, encouragement, comfort, or
simply helping to move the classroom chairs. Each leaf
may or may not have the name of the child who did the

giving on it. Perhaps better than competing for the
most giving person, children could write the good deed
itself on the leaf. As a joint project, the tree will soon
be laden with leaves, and the classroom will be bubbling
with good will, as the children discover the fun of giving.
(If this is to be a one-day project, simply draw the tree
on a blackboard and add the leaves as deserved.)

31 ★ dePAOLA, Tomie. Strega Nona. Prentice-Hall, 1975.

This is an old Italian folktale of the village witch
Strega Nona and her magic potions and cures. She
hired Big Anthony to look after her house and garden,
but he overheard one of her secret spells. He rushed
off to try the magic, and the trouble began when he
didn't see what Strega Nona did to stop the spell. Soon
the entire town was inundated with spaghetti from the
magic pot.

Activities

1) Read the story aloud to the point where Big Anthony
is being punished. Ask the children if they can think of
a good punishment for Big Anthony. Guide the younger
children into logical thinking concerning punishments.
Discuss the qualities that Strega Nona possessed to
make her a good witch. Even though the townspeople
were afraid of her, they came to her for cures and re-
spected her wisdom in the punishment.
Was Big Anthony really bad? Or was he just curious?
Ask the children how many of them would like to try some
magic. What child could resist the temptation?

2) Ask the children to close their eyes after the story is
over. Picture a good witch--remember, she doesn't have
to be beautiful to be good. Now think of a good name for
your witch. She must have something magic in her house
and a good spell. Ask the children to draw their witch
and tell a story of her magic. Point out that a rhyme
can help a witch remember her spell better.

32 ★ DIAMOND, Donna. The Pied Piper of Hamlin. Holiday
         House, 1981.

Here is a beautifully illustrated prose version of the

famous narrative poem in which the Pied Piper, who
rid the town of Hamlin of its rats but was refused the
payment promised by the Town Council.   He then played
his pipe and all of the children of the town followed him
through the mountains, never to return!   A classic that
should be introduced to all children.

Activities

1) Discuss: If we agree to do something for someone,
why is it important that we keep our promise?
   Have the children write a message to themselves,
telling one thing that they like about themselves and one
that they promise to do for someone else this year.
Have them seal it in an envelope and put their names
on the outside.   Then collect the envelopes.   In a week
or month, or at the end of the year, deliver it back to
them and let them privately reread it.   Was the promise
kept?

2) Let the children make their own stationery.   This can
be done by gluing a strip of colored construction paper
down one edge of a piece of paper.   On top of this, dried
leaves or flowers or construction-paper designs can be
glued.   Another idea is to make a leaf rubbing in the
corner.   This can be done by placing a leaf or design
cut out of cardboard under a sheet of paper.   Then with
a crayon rub on top of it and a design appears.

33 ★ DIAMOND, Donna.   Swan Lake.   Adapted from the ballet
        by Pëtr Ilich Tchaikovsky.   Holiday House, 1980.

   Using the rich imagery and language of a Russian
fairytale, Donna Diamond tells and illustrates the classic ballet as a story.   Odette, the Swan Queen, lived
her days as a bird but at night became a beautiful woman.
The spell could be broken only if a man pledged to love
her, marry her, and never love another.   When a prince
discovered her by a moonlit lake, he fell in love with
her, a love that was doomed from the beginning.   This
is a beautiful introduction to the ballet and should be introduced with the music.

Activities

1) Discuss the following: What does it mean to be

possessive?   What examples of possessiveness are evident in this story?   Can possessiveness lead to bigger
problems?   In what ways does Tchaikovsky bring this
story to life in music?   Which scenes were most vivid
to you as you listened to the music?

2) Brainstorm: Tickle the imaginations of the class.
Try to name as many uses of a feather as possible.
    Find books in the library about swans.   Where are
they usually found?   What are their habits?   Did you
find any of these in the story?

34 ★ DILLON, Barbara.   Who Needs a Bear?   Illustrated by
        Diane de Groat.   Morrow, 1981.

    Memorably drawn characters distinguish this tale of
three toys who leave their attic limbo to search for a
new home.   Malcolm, a teddy bear, is the natural leader
as he is the oldest.   Gwendolyn, a petulant doll, and Apple, an excitable stuffed monkey, complete the trio.
Once outdoors, the toys proceed--despite an encounter
with a rambunctious dog--to the park, where first Gwendolyn and then Apple find new companions.   But who
wants an old, tired bear?   Malcolm must endure lone-
liness and other trials before he is taken into a home
so perfect that he couldn't possibly have dreamed it.

Activity

    The characters in this story took an unexpected trip
and were not prepared for it.   Choose one place in the
United States, Canada, or Mexico you have never been.
Read about that place in books from your school library.
Plan a trip to the place.   Answer these questions in
your planning.

    a) Where I want to go _____

    b) Best means to travel _____

    c) Lowest cost means of travel _____

    d) Travel time by car _____ plane _____.
        other _____

    e) What I need to take _____

    f) How long I will be gone _____

g) Sights I want to see _____

h) Estimated budget for the trip:

   transportation _____ lodging _____

   food _____ sightseeing _____

   other _____

i) Problems to prepare for _____

35 ★ DORROS, Arthur. <u>Pretzels.</u> Greenwillow, 1981.

   Here is an imaginative, easy-to-read tale about the
origin of a favorite snack: pretzels. Here children
meet the hilarious crew of the ship <u>Bungle</u>, from absent-
minded Captain Fast to First Mate Pretzel. The ship
also boasts the sea's worst cook, I Fryem Fine, and
Max, the cabin boy who becomes the hero of the tale.
Children will discover along with these unusual characters an even more unusual land!

<u>Activities</u>

1) A variety of pretzels can easily be brought into the
classroom for a pretzel-tasting party. Many children
may even be pleasantly surprised to discover a new
taste or shape. If you're lucky, you can visit and tour
a bakery (or even better--a pretzel factory) with the
children. A firsthand look at the process might better
explain the tough job that Walter had.

2) After the children have been exposed to a sampling
of pretzels actually available, let them create their own
pretzels from clay. Everyone can begin by working the
clay into one long roll. Then encourage the children to
let their imaginations invent a brand new twist. Remember, if they're not satisfied, they can just begin again.
After drying, the new pretzels can be hung by string
from hangers to make several "twisted" mobiles.

3) At some point in the intermediate grades it is fun
to have students work with folktales. Explain simply
that folktales are stories that come from early times;
sometimes they are about imaginary heroes and sometimes about how something got to be the way it is.
After reading and sharing the story of Walter, explain
that this is Mr. Dorros's version of how the pretzel
came into existence.

   With brown wrapping paper and white tempera paint,
have students make two copies of a pretzel. (See sample.) When dry, put some sheets of paper between and
staple, making a small story booklet. While children's
pretzels are drying, have them write an original story
about how they think the pretzel was invented. Copy
corrected stories into pretzel booklets and display with
the caption "A NEW TWIST."

36 ★ FAIR, Sylvia. The Bedspread. Morrow, 1982.

   A magnificent embroidered bedspread and how it comes
to be is the theme of this strongly visual picture book.
Artfully it explores in a fresh way the perennial interest
of children in the "olden times" of a family. Maud and
Amelia are two old sisters who each live at one end of
a long, long bed. Although they disagree about most
things, they do agree that their plain white bedspread is
the most boring feature of their boring life. So they decide to decorate it, each embroidering on it their recol-
lection of the house in which they grew up. When finished,
the bedspread is a surprise that each sister treasures in
her own way.

Activities

1) Ask students to list events in their lives that they most
want to remember. Fold a sheet of paper in half three
times, yielding eight boxes. In each box draw an object
(or cut and paste a picture from an old magazine) that
recalls each event. Display the "memory boxes" for all
to see and discuss.

2) The two sisters in this story would have given meanings to these words different from those we would give
today. Can you discover what each word meant fifty
years ago? a) syrup; b) parson; c) salute; d) whitewash;
e) do; f) study.

37 ★ FLORIAN, Douglas. The City. Crowell, 1982.

     Young students will explore a big and busy city through the pages of this wordless picture book. From the first double-page spread of the rooftops, the artist takes children across busy bridges, down wide avenues, past construction sites, into a subway, through busy shopping centers, to quiet parks, and finally home to a high-rise apartment. It is truly a book for viewing and discussing.

Activities

1) Words Make Pictures. Ask each student to select one object usually found in a large city. Make a list of words to describe the object. Use the words to create a picture of the object.

<pre>
                    O
              T   P

              HIGH   MANY FLOORS
              TALL,

           B U I L D I N G
</pre>

2) Discuss:

    a) All the good things about living in a big city.
    b) All the good things about living in a small town.
    c) All the good things about living in the country.
    d) Where would you choose to live?

38 ★ GAMMELL, Stephen.   Once Upon MacDonald's Farm.
     Four Winds, 1981.

     Everyone knows that MacDonald had a farm. But how did he get those animals that neigh and cluck and moo in the popular song? Stephen Gammell wondered, and then he began to write this funny story. Plucky

MacDonald is eager to work at some farm chores.   So
he buys an elephant, a lion, and a baboon.   The plowing,
milking, and egg-gathering do not go well, and, to make
matters worse, the animals are disgusted with MacDonald's lack of know-how.   They run away during the night.
Fortunately a wise and practical neighbor is charitable.
He gives MacDonald a horse, a cow, and a hen.   Our
farmer is ready to try again.   With the hen harnessed
to the plow and a whole field ahead, he sighs with con-
tentment: "Ee-i-oh. "

Activities

1) There are many jobs to be done on a farm.   Have
a brainstorming session to see how many the class can
name.   List the jobs on the board.

2) Divide the class into groups of four or five.   Ask
each group to select a moderator and a recorder.   Each
group will have fifteen minutes to decide on one of the
jobs listed on the board and to come up with an easier
way to do the job than the way in which it is normally
done.   No magic allowed, but a bit of tall-tale exaggeration is permitted!

39 ★ GASCOIGNE, Bamber.   Why the Rope Went Tight.
      Illustrated by Christina Gascoigne.   Lothrop, Lee
      & Shepard, 1981.

Here is a modern "chain-of-events" story that tells
why the rope went tight.   Text and illustrations take
the reader along the rope's path from a small boy to
a man, to a girl, to a pedigree dog, past Spruce Bruce
and Saucy Sal, along to a host of other circus performers to end with "Lickchop Leo, the fiercest, greediest,
and most generally rumptious and bumptious lion" the
circus has ever known.   A fable complete with a moral
and a colorful introduction to the circus world.

Activities

1) To follow up on the idea of one event leading to another, divide the class into several groups.   Allow time
for each group to develop its own chain-of-events story,
which can then be told "round robin" fashion to the class.
Encourage children to stretch their imaginations in the

telling and to think of colorful words and phrases to
describe the setting of their story.

2) Circus wagons can brighten any classroom!   Each
child can make a circus wagon and cage an animal.
Start with a light-colored 9"x12" sheet of construction
paper.   Turn the paper horizontally and have each child
draw and color (or cut out and glue) an animal in the
cage.   Cut black yarn into 9" strips.   These can be
glued at the top and bottom for bars.   Finally, cut out
and glue a colorfully decorated cage-top and two wheels.
All cages can be connected when finished.

3) Sequential order is an important skill in listening
as well as in writing, and one in which some middle
graders are especially weak.   This book, though very
elementary, can definitely help children understand sequence.   Follow up with a little more difficult sequenc-
ing activity.   Bring in several sections of the comics
from the daily newspaper.   Have students select a
comic strip that has no more than seven frames.   Give
the children envelopes and have them cut the strip out
and cut each frame apart.   Then they can trade envelopes and put the strips in sequential order, checking
each other.

40 ★ GEORGE, Jean Craighead. The Grizzly Bear with the
      Golden Ears.   Illustrated by Tom Cantina.   Harper
      & Row, 1982.

      As a young bear living by the salmon-rich Brooks
River in Alaska, Golden Ears plays a game of bluffing
other bears into giving up their catch--which she finds
easier than having to catch her own fish.   When she
begins to threaten humans and to teach her cub to do
the same, the park ranger fears the bear will have to
be taught a painful lesson.   Then, one day, upon returning from a fish-stealing expedition, Golden Ears discovers that her cub is gone, leaving behind only his
scent, mixed with that of the enormous male, Ursus.
"All night Golden Ears searched the river bank.   She
woofed and cried and suffered. ...   In the morning,
Golden Ears gave up the hunt.   She walked in silence. "
With the sure insight of a superb naturalist, Jean Craighead George tells a suspenseful tale of the Far North
and deepens children's knowledge and understanding of
wildlife.

Activity

      The author has made numerous trips to Alaska and
describes the Brooks River setting with accurate detail.
To help students see the importance of detail, ask them
to choose a familiar setting (their own room at home,
a favorite place to play) and to write a detailed description of it.   Consider:

      a) What objects would be seen?
      b) Weather (if applicable), temperature?
      c) Major colors, patterns, shapes?
      d) Sounds and smells?
      e) What would one most remember after visiting this
         place?

41 ★ GIVENS, Janet.   Something Wonderful Happened.   Illus-
      trated by Susan Dodge.   Atheneum, 1982.

      Millions and millions of years ago this planet we
call earth was without flowers.   It was the age of dino-
saurs, which lumbered over land and swam in shallow
seas.   Then, one day, something wonderful happened!
A flower bloomed, and from it came the very first

seeds.   Each seed held a tiny new plant with enough
food around it to help it grow.   Birds, insects, and
all sorts of animals found this earth a good place to
live because of the flowers and their seeds.   This
poetic text and detailed illustrations reflect the very
young child's sense of wonder for the natural world.

Activities

1) The common but effective growth of a lima bean can
allow children to view the rooting process firsthand.
Give each child one lima bean, one dampened paper
towel, one plastic bag, and tape.   Instruct them to put
the bean on the towel, place it in the bag, and tape on
their desks.   They can witness a miracle of their own.

2) This book spells out in simplified terms the vital
role of seeds.   It would be especially good to use during a study of seed dispersal.   Make a large chart to
use in the room and have the class chart and classify
the following seeds by their method of dispersal: witch
hazel, cocklebur, milkweed, geranium, dandelion, coconut, cottonwood, orchid, maple, lotus, water lily,
poppy seeds, sycamore, acorn, ash, hyacinth, pecan,
star thistle   (see chart below).   Then challenge students
to bring in little-known facts about seeds.   Example:
the coconut is the largest seed.   This will encourage
the use of reference books.

SEED DISPERSAL			
Animals	Exploding Pods	Water	Wind

42 ★ GOODALL, John S. Paddy's New Hat. Atheneum,
       1980.

     In this delightful, wordless picture book for all ages,
Paddy Pig chases his just-purchased, wind-blown new
hat into a police recruiting station, where the Sergeant
signs him up. But Paddy has much to learn about being a policeman! Handcuffed to a burglar twice his size,
he winds up face down in a rain barrel. Assigned to
direct traffic, he creates a terrible traffic jam. Finally,
encountering a robber, Paddy shows his true bravery and
saves the day. Rich, colorful, highly detailed illustrations make this a visual delight and a wonderful book for
oral interpretation.

Activities

1) Set up a wordless-picture-book display in the classroom and encourage children to view the books carefully.
Ask for volunteers to interpret orally a favorite book to
the class or to a small group within the class.

2) This book is an excellent example of the power of
pictures to communicate ideas and stories. The illustrations must be studied at a leisurely pace in order not
to miss minute details important to the story. Students
may want to develop their own wordless stories to share
with others. Ask students to save the daily newspaper
comics for several days. These can be "mixed and
matched" as parts of various comics (without captions)
to tell a picture story. Students should try interpreting
orally each other's finished stories. (Portions of comics
should be cut out and glued on another sheet of paper in
whatever sequence the student desires.)

43 ★ GWYNNE, Fred. The Sixteen Hand Horse. Windmill,
       1980.

     Actor Fred Gwynne has added this third title to his
popular series of books that play with words. The first
two were The King Who Rained (Windmill, 1970; see
the first edition of E IS FOR EVERYBODY, page 31)
and A Chocolate Moose for Dinner (Windmill, 1976).
Seen through a child's literal interpretation, these are
books that play with homonyms. This third title should
become as much a favorite as the first two.

Activities

1) Older boys and girls will have fun developing their
own word pictures based on homographs and homonyms.
This is an excellent book to use in introducing the idea
of words that sound the same but have different meanings.

2) Younger students can be challenged to see how many
words they can find in their pictionaries that have the
same sound but different meanings.   This idea can be
developed into a word game.   One child can say a word
and give one meaning, then call on another child to give
a different meaning.   If the second child answers correctly, he or she can begin with a new word.

44 ★ HASTINGS, Selina.   Sir Gawain and the Green Knight.
      Illustrated by Juan Wijngaard.   Lothrop, Lee &
      Shepard, 1981.

      Young Sir Gawain, as yet an untried knight at King
Arthur's Round Table, eagerly accepted the challenge of
the superhuman Green Knight and rode off alone to meet
it.   His journey was filled with danger and hardship and
apprehension at the trial ahead.   But at the end of his
journey he was met by an altogether different kind of
test from the one he had anticipated, and he came away
wiser for having learned that a true knight must have
more than one kind of strength.   Richly detailed, boldly
colored illustrations enhance this legendary tale of chiv-
alry, retold in modern English.

Activities

1) How many other heroes can students name who follow
the basic folktale-hero pattern: that is, a) young hero
is honest, kind, and brave; b) travels alone; c) seeks
adventure; d) is given task to perform or danger to
overcome; e) meets obstacles; f) sometimes helped by
others; g) succeeds in task; h) rewarded in some way.
Remind students of Taran from The High King or of
Luke Skywalker from Star Wars to begin their thinking
about folk heroes.

2) Acrostic Poetry: In thinking about the qualities or
characteristics of Sir Gawain and of the Green Knight,
challenge students to write a descriptive acrostic poem
about each.   Here are some beginnings!

Sir Gawain and the Green Knight (illustration © 1981 by Juan Wijngaard)

Sincere	Gave his head to the sword
Initiated action	Revenge
Revealed his weakness	Elaborate costume
G	E
A	N
W	K
A	N
I	I
N	G
	H
	T

45 ★ HEIDE, Florence Parry. Treehorn's Treasure. Illustrated by Edward Gorey. Holiday House, 1981.

Treehorn lives out of his closet, where he keeps his comic books, baseball cards, bubble gum, and other daily needs. One day Treehorn discovers that money really does grow on trees, or at least on one tree in his yard. When he tried to share his discovery with others, he is ignored, but as in The Shrinking of Treehorn he once again solves his own problems.

Activities

1) Class members might compile a Book of Spells designed to cure one or more of the world's ills. Each student should list the ingredients and procedure for using his or her "spell" as well as its intended effect.

2) Primary children can have a special browsing time in the school library to see how many books they can find for their classroom reading table on witches and wizards. During the browsing time encourage children to choose another book about real people. Stress the idea that books can tell about both real and imaginary things.

3) Have students compose a cinquain about their favorite character in the book. A cinquain is a five line poem constructed as follows:

1st line	1 word--noun	Boy,
2nd line	2 words that describe	curious, questioning,
3rd line	3 words showing action	discovers, tells, acts;
4th line	4 words showing feeling	comments ignored by all:
5th line	1 word, synonym for line 1	Treehorn.

46 ★ HENKES, Kevin. All Alone. Greenwillow, 1981.

When you are alone, you can do all sorts of things-- pretend you are tiny or huge, hear things other people can't hear, and see things they can't see. You can think of favorite things you have done and even ask yourself questions you can't answer. "When I'm alone I look at myself inside and out. No one looks just like me or thinks just like I do." Children who enjoy being alone will see themselves in this book and those who do not

may enjoy the feeling of quiet for just a little while.
A thoughtful and introspective book.

Activities

1) After children have viewed the author's pictures of
"quiet," ask them to listen carefully to the sounds
around them. Use a tape recorder and blank tape to
record the sounds the children can hear even when the
class is quiet. Have the students check their answers
as to what they heard during this listening period with
the sounds recorded on the tape.

2) Distribute old magazines that can be cut up. Ask
each student to find pictures that would fit well into a
"Quiet Collage." Students should cut and arrange pictures on construction paper and title their collage with
their own definition of "quiet." Some students may pre-
fer to concentrate on the idea of "silent activity." Children can search the classroom or playground for signs
of silent activity. Some students can include in their
collage such things as plants growing or a bug crawling
along the baseboard.

3) Children should be encouraged to find a picture from
nature, draw a picture or photograph one element of a
nature scene. Each child should then determine the one
word that best describes the object. For example: A
child who has photographed or drawn a rabbit might
choose the word "soft." Using the dictionary of synonyms or the thesaurus, the children should find as many
words as they can that might be used to describe their
pictures. Some children might desire to set these words
up in a rhythmic or rhyming pattern to be used in cap-
tioning their pictures.

47 ★ HICKMAN, Martha Whitmore. The Reason I'm Not Quite
        Finished Tying My Shoes. Illustrated by Jim Padgett.
        Abingdon, 1981.

It's almost time for school and Annamaria has not
quite finished tying her shoes. What if someone comes
over and she has to stop in the middle? Her thumb
could get caught in the loops and she might not be able
to get it out. If her shoes were on, she couldn't reach
her toes if they started to itch! Lively, fluent excuses

and bright pictures help children realize they are not
the only ones who have trouble getting started in the
morning!

Activities

1) Discuss: What is so wonderful about feeling happy?
   What things have you recently learned to do for
yourself?
   What's nice about a smile?
   If you were asked to help your brother or sister tie
their shoes, what would you say or do?

2) This is an excellent story for the children to act out
in mime as you read or narrate.

3) Create a "Someone Assignment." This can consist
of various projects for the children to complete, for
example:

   a) Help someone to laugh.
   b) Show someone how nice she is.
   c) Share a smile with someone you pass.
   d) Give someone something special, e.g., a hug, a
      wildflower, a pinecone, a homemade card, a
      decorated box.
   e) Make someone a card, perhaps with a tin-foil
      mirror inside, listing some of his most enjoyable
      qualities.

48 ★ HIGHWATER, Jamake. Moonsong Lullaby. Photographs
     by Marcia Keegan. Lothrop, Lee & Shepard, 1981.

      The moon watching over the night is an important
theme in Native American lore. It is said that the
moon sings to soothe the sleep of the sun as she makes
her path across the night sky. Here is an original lullaby on this theme inspired by early American Indian
stories. Illustrated with photographs to capture the
reader's eye and imagination.

Activities

1) Older children can list facts learned about a people
they have studied and try to produce their own class
ABC book. Each child can be assigned one letter and

find and explain a word or term in either prose or poetry. Each letter (and word) should be illustrated. If
possible, pages should be laminated and bound together
with metal rings and the finished book given to the library for enjoyment by other students.

2) Primary students can compile a "School ABC Book,"
which can be placed in the school library for new students to see. Each letter should represent one important word that can be used in a simple sentence as a
caption for a student illustration concerning some aspect
of school life.

3) Though the format of the book appears to be quite
simple, it is not intended for very young readers. It
is, however, a beautiful blend of text and photography
and should inspire young camera buffs to attempt their
own creative photographic essays. Children should be
cautioned to keep first attempts simple--two or three
photographs, related in some way and accompanied by
original text in either prose or poetry. If children do
not have cameras available, perhaps the loan of a camera can be arranged and each child be allowed to take
one or two pictures around the school. Sometimes
funds can be obtained from PTA groups for purchase
and processing of film.

49 ★ HOBAN, Tana. Take Another Look. Greenwillow, 1981.

        Here is a delightful sequel to the author's popular
Look Again (Macmillan, 1971). A see-through window
on one page allows the child a partial image of the
photograph on the next page. All kinds of surprises
are in store as the reader guesses what is in store.
See-through windows are arranged so that the book can
be viewed forward or backward.

Activities

1) Check with the library for books to place in the classroom reading corner that will challenge children to examine illustrations for color, texture, shape, form, and
detail. Among the best are books by Mitsumasa Anno,
whose Anno's Journey and Anno's Italy are visual challenges for students of all ages. Collect, too, many of
the wordless picture books of John Goodall and Mercer
Mayer.

2) Distribute construction paper and old magazines.
Children can find pictures rich in pattern or texture
and make their own "Look Again" pages. What fun
when classmates try to stump each other to "Take
Another Look!"

50 ★ HOFFMAN, Rosekrans. Sister Sweet Ella. Morrow,
         1982.

Here is a funny lesson in learning to look at a variety of alternatives before deciding on the best solution
to a problem! Everyone loves Sister Sweet Ella--that
is, everyone but Wadsworth. Mama dotes on her; perfect strangers offer her jellybeans; dogs stand on their
hind legs to see her better. Goaded beyond endurance,
Wadsworth casts a spell to turn Ella into a cat, an animal Mama hates. Ella disappears, and a scraggly cat
turns up in her place. Wadsworth is pleased, certain
that now he and Mama can be happy together again.
But he discovers that finding a home for the motley-
looking creature isn't so easy. People once charmed
by Baby Ella are not entranced by a homely cat. Almost too late, Wadsworth comes to the realization that
dabbling in magic can be a very risky business.

Activities

1) Suppose you had a cat you wanted someone else to
take. Design a "FOR SALE" advertisement extolling
the many benefits of being a cat owner. Be positive--
how many things can you think of?

2) Select an unusual animal (tarantula, platypus). Design a want ad to sell your animal. Example:

             Porcupine for sale! Cheap!
             Have at your fingertips a
             creature that will:
             Provide an endless supply of
             writing quills!
             Save your seat at the movies
             while you go for popcorn!

51 ★ HOPKINS, Lee Bennett. I Am the Cat. Illustrated by
         Linda Richards. Harcourt Brace Jovanovich, 1981.

Here is a diverse collection of poems about cats by an impressive array of writers, including T. S. Eliot, Kay Starbird, Myra Cohn Livingston, and Eleanor Farjeon. Children will meet marmalade cats, spotted cats, white cats, the old Tom cat, bird watchers, and a host of others, all illustrated with beautifully detailed line drawings. Poetry for every mood to stimulate the imagination and delight the ear!

Activities

1) The door has been opened for a science lesson on the cat kingdom. The illustrator has pictured a wide variety of cats, large and small. A study of cats both tame and wild, with beginning use of the encyclopedia for young children, can give background information for a study of similarities and differences in cat characteristics and habitats.

2) A simple shape for a cat can be made by simply folding a piece of construction paper in half and cutting a half-circle from the middle. Using construction paper and glue, or crayons, add other features (head, tail, etc.). The colors and decorations can be chosen in relation to the cat selected. When completed, the cats of the world stand ready to greet all with a gentle purr or a fierce roar.

3) This book could be used as an introduction to well-known books with famous cat characters. Have groups of students research this, using the subject card catalog in the library. Prepare a bulletin board with the caption "WHERE IS MY CAT?" Tape together, along one long edge, two 8"x10" cards. On the top card write a

question by an author and sign the author's name. By lifting the flap, students learn the name of the book where the cat can be found.   Here are some examples:

a) Alice met my cat, but he slowly disappeared except for his grin, which stayed for a long time after he was gone.   Where can I find my Cheshire cat?
signed: Lewis Carroll
answer under flap: Alice in Wonderland

My cat set out to sea in a pea-green boat.   She was accompanied by an owl.   Where can I find my cat?
signed: Edward Lear
answer under flap: "The Owl and the Pussy Cat" (poem)

Other stories that might be used: "The Black Cat," by Edgar Allan Poe; "Puss in Boots," by Charles Perrault; "Cricket in Times Square," by George Selden; "The Duel," by Eugene Field.

52 ★ HOUSTON, James.   Long Claws: An Arctic Adventure.
Atheneum, 1981.

After their father's death, it was a starvation winter for Pitohok, his sister, Upik, and their family.   Frozen lake trout that they found, with the help of a snow owl, provided their first food in three days.   Then the children set out on an arduous journey to dig up a frozen caribou, buried by their grandfather.   To be alone on the vast, frozen tundra was frightening enough, but their fright turned to terror when a huge grizzly bear, known as Long Claws, picked up their homeward trail and followed to steal the meat.   How could they fight him off? Yet to give up meant death by starvation.   This dramatic story, told by a master storyteller, will hold its readers spellbound.

Activities

1) Arctic A-Z: You will need one sheet of white paper and crayons.   Draw curved lines on your paper to make twenty-six spaces (a).   Put one letter of the alphabet in each space (b).   For each letter draw one thing found in the Arctic beginning with that letter (c).

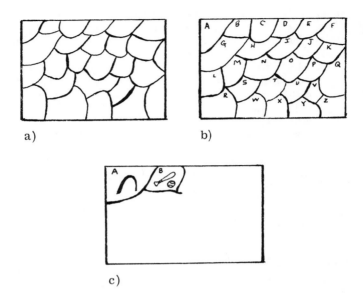

a)   b)

c)

2) Upper-grade students who study other countries of the world will find this an appealing way to present information rather than being required to produce the traditional written report. Students can research important cultural, economic, and historical facts about a particular country and present this information as their own colorful alphabet book.

3) A primary class can compile a class alphabet based on concepts concerning their school, town, or home.

53 ★ HUTCHINS, Pat. <u>1 Hunter</u>. Greenwillow, 1982.

    The pictures rather than the words tell this cumulative tale. One hunter walks through the jungle. He does not see TWO elephants, or THREE giraffes, or FOUR ostriches, but they see him. Following the clues on each page to the next group of animals that will appear, young counters take a true adventure walk as they discover animals in groups of one to ten. The reader's surprise will match that of the hunter as, on the next-to-last page, he turns to discover all of the jungle animals following him!

Activities

1) How many animals would you expect to find on the next-to-last page? (An older brother or sister may have to help here.) Count and see if the artist has included all of them.

2) Suppose the hunter became lost in the jungle. Let the children design their own rescue kits. They can draw, color, and cut out all sorts of items to include in their kits (perhaps a shoe box or smaller container).

3) Keep your eye out for possible hiking places. This will enable everyone to be able to work together in the planning an actual excursion (expedition). Perhaps the class can put together their own "gorp" (hiking food). This is a mixture usually consisting of "M&Ms" and any kind of nuts, peanuts, coconut, raisins, or sunflower seeds--the selection is endless.

54 ★ ISADORA, Rachel. Ben's Trumpet. Greenwillow, 1979.

The story of Ben is fiction, but it could be the story of more than one jazz musician who grew up in the twenties. Using the Art Deco style of the period, the author-artist captures the poignancy and yearning of youthful talent as Ben listens to the jazz musicians and feels the rhythm all the way home. His pretend trumpet satisfies his longing in part to be a musician, until he is laughed at by the local gang: "He sets on the stoop and watches the blinking lights of the Zig Zag Jazz Club. He sits there a long time, just watching." And then the miracle happens!

Activities

1) Experiment with images gained through music. On one day you might deal only with objects. Have ready several musical selections that suggest one or two specific objects. Listen to a portion of each selection (with eyes closed) and then discuss. Finally, distribute drawing paper to the children. Tell them to listen again and draw a simple picture of what the music means to them. Follow the same procedure on other days using colors, shapes, moods, etc.

2) A simple yet effective method of transforming music into art is through a scribble drawing. If the previous activity is used, the children will have trained themselves to listen to the music as a whole and also as separate parts. The scribble drawing merely combines the parts to produce a whole image. Provide a musical selection that has at least one change of tempo. A short selection will work best. Instruct the children to use a black crayon and let the music guide the crayon on the paper in one continuous stroke. If a specific object comes to mind, the rough outline of that object can be drawn (again in one stroke). Have them color in all spaces. Finally, let each child tell what he or she "saw in the song."

3) Discuss collages with students and then share this book. Elicit discussion about "seeing" music and what type of music one might have heard to produce the collages in the book. Talk about the way we normally "see"--through the eyes.
    Next play for students a musical selection that has a lot of variety. Tell students to think about the one word that this music makes them feel. After listening, students should write their word on a piece of manila paper. Then they are to make a "word collage." Have them look for the letters of their word in magazines and newspapers. Cut out several of each letter and arrange them into the spelling of their own word several times on a piece of construction paper, pasting the letters in place. Display the finished collages and then again play the musical selection so that everyone can appreciate the way others "saw" this particular piece of music.

55 ★ KALEN, Robert. Jump, Frog, Jump. Illustrated by
        Byron Barton. Greenwillow, 1981.

    Here is a cumulative tale that poses a problem on every page. "This is the turtle that slid into the pond and ate the snake that dropped from a branch and swallowed the fish that swam after the frog--Jump, Frog, Jump!" Jumping at just the right time does seem to solve most of frog's problems, until he is captured by some boys and imprisoned under a large basket. Jumping won't help frog to escape, but something else does! Bright, bold pictures and cliff-hanger anticipation should make this a sure winner with primary children and a delightful patterning model for older students.

Jump, Frog, Jump (illustration © 1981 by Byron Barton)

Activities

1) If a portable tape recorder is available, the teacher
can record the sounds in a wooded area. Play the tape
and see how many sounds children can identify. Have
students suggest other creatures that belong in a woodland or pond setting and find out what kind of sound each
creature makes.

2) Ask each child to choose one of the woodland or pond
sounds heard in the story. The class can then give its
own woodland concert--perhaps in conjunction with a music class, where a soft piano accompaniment can be
added. The "concert" might be recorded on tape so that
the class can hear how they sound.

3) Let each child secretly choose to be one animal. In
order to discover the habits of the animal, a library
visit may be necessary, or before the story is read a
collection of animal books suitable for your grade level
could be borrowed from the library for the classroom
reading table. After the children have discovered facts
about the habits of their animals, allow them (one at a
time) to pantomime the animals for others to guess.
Each child might also tell the class which animal trait
would be the most difficult (or impossible) for a human
to imitate.

56 ★ KEATS, Ezra Jack.   Kitten for a Day.   Four Winds,
        1982.

        Four playful kittens and a good-natured and friendly

(but somewhat confused) puppy add up to a day of fun
for all. When the kittens invite the pup to join them in
their play, not even a bumped nose and a little spilled
milk can dampen his spirits. The pup's mother eventually takes him home, but not before he has found some
new friends, with the promise of another day of play before them. Ezra Jack Keats substitutes color and form
for words in this happy picture book, enabling even the
youngest reader to become a participant in the fun.

Activities

1) In this story the puppy didn't know he was a puppy.
Using the pattern found in Margaret Wise Brown's The
Important Book (Harper & Row, 1949), write descrip-
tions of a) a puppy and b) a kitten. How do they differ?
The pattern is as follows:

"The important thing about an apple is that it is
round. You bite it and it is white inside, and it tastes
like an apple and it falls from a tree. But the important thing about an apple is that it is round."

2) Share A Tree Is Nice, by Janice Udry (Harper &
Row, 1956). Elaborate on the pattern by writing a class
language-experience story: "A Puppy Is Nice" or "A
Kitten Is Nice."

57 ★ KEATS, Ezra Jack. Regards to the Man in the Moon.
        Four Winds, 1981.

        Louis was being teased by the kids because his pop
was a junkman. His father's rejoinder was that with
junk and a little imagination, a person can go "right
out of this world." Spurred by this thought, Louis and
his friend built a spacecraft fueled entirely by imagination. Their escapades in the stratosphere provided both
wonder and fear. The next day, when the other kids
heard about their adventures, they too wanted to take
off on imagination, as will the children with whom this
delightful picture book is shared.

Activities

1) Missing Object: Make available to the class one or
more large pictures that show action. Ask students to

imagine an object that is missing in the picture. Draw
or write a description of the missing object. Use your
imagination! Tell what the object is, what it looks like,
why it belongs in the picture.

2) Ask students to find an action picture in an old magazine and bring to class. Cover up half of the picture
with blank paper. Students exchange pictures and use
their imaginations to tell or write what each imagines
to be in the missing half.

58 ★ KENNEDY, Richard. The Lost Kingdom of Karnica.
    Illustrated by Uri Shulevitz. Sierra Club/Scribner,
    1979.

Before the stone was found, the land of the Kingdom
of Karnica was rich and yielding. But when a farmer
digging a well discovered the rich red stone, the King
was determined that the land should give up its riches
even though the wise man predicted disaster if "the
heart of the kingdom" were removed. Heedless to the
warning, the people rushed to dig up the stone and, as
a result, destroyed their kingdom. This is a story to
be read and discussed on many levels.

Activities

1) While this may seem an imaginary take-off on an important subject, children will quickly get the message
that only people can do something about their own environment. Discussion of the kinds of pollution (noise,
air, water, etc.) can lead children to a greater awareness of the problem. Ask students to watch their newspapers for one week and to bring to class any articles
they find concerning the efforts of the government, conservation groups, or individual citizens to improve the
environment and to fight pollution. Post these articles
in a "Recreate the Karnica" corner of the class bulletin
board for all class members to read.

2) Divide the class into two debating teams. Give one
team the responsibility for supporting an affirmative
answer to the question "Is Progress Always Good?" The
second team will take the negative view. Stress that de-
baters must have more than their own views to present
in a debate.

3) Ask primary children what animals or birds they
see around their homes or on trips they make to the
country.   If the school subscribes to <u>Ranger Rick</u> magazine, borrow back issues for the classroom reading
table.   When children have had time to look through
the magazines, ask them what they saw people doing to
take care of wild animals?   What can they do to pre-
serve our natural environment?   Post the list of class
suggestions on the bulletin board.

4) Students can discuss ways in which they can make
their school a more beautiful place for others to enjoy.
Such discussion can result in action decided upon by the
class--perhaps the planting of flowers in some part of
the school grounds or the painting of a mural on library
or cafeteria walls.   If painting is not possible, a burlap
wall hanging with attractive stitchery can be hung in
some area of the school to make it more attractive.
Students will have many other ideas.

59 ★ KNOTTS, Howard.   <u>The Summer Cat</u>.   Harper & Row,
       1981.

    A beautiful calico cat mysteriously appears in the
apple tree in the evening and is gone by day.   Ben, who
names her Apple Blossom, considers her his own.   Then
he discovers that she already has a home.   "I'm going
to make her love me more than that summer lady, " Ben
tells his sister, Annie.   "Then she'll stay here. "   But
when it's almost fall, Apple Blossom doesn't come around
for four days.   And Annie realizes why not even the summer lady can find the cat.   In this delicately illustrated
companion to <u>The Winter Cat</u> a young boy learns that,
though he loves it very much, he cannot keep something
belonging to someone else.

Activities

1) Discuss: Have you ever found something that you
knew belonged to someone else?   What did you do?
    Have you ever lost something that you treasured?
Was it returned to you?   How did you feel when you
lost it?
    Where is the first place you would look for a lost
pet?
    Are there agencies in your community that take care
of lost or unwanted animals?

The Summer Cat

Why are people who live in the city cautioned not to take their unwanted pets and dump them out in a country meadow or woods?

2) In this story there are many moods that can be shown by colors. Discuss the relationship of colors to mood. Challenge children to tell the story by drawing geometric shapes of various colors in the order in which the moods occur. Ask several students to explain their color story outlines.

60 ★ KRAHN, Fernando. The Creepy Thing. Houghton
      Mifflin/Clarion, 1982.

A little boy sets out one day to catch a fish, but what he hooks is an unappetizing stringy thing. He tosses it away and sits down to play his harmonica. Then the creepy thing begins to dance to his music. Delighted, the boy takes his new friend home with him. During the night, the creepy thing escapes. The next day it

terrorizes the town until the police surround it, prepared to shoot it down. Can the boy find a way to save
his friend? Here is a delightful problem-solving situation for the very youngest, who should, if they are careful listeners, pick up clues in the story to help the
young hero solve his problem.

Activity

Share the story to the point where the police are
prepared to shoot the creepy thing. Through class
discussion follow this problem-solving procedure:

a) State the facts leading to the problem.
b) State the problem.
c) Brainstorm for solutions (alternatives).
d) State what you want the solution to accomplish
   (criteria).
e) Examine each alternative in light of your criteria.
f) Choose the best solution.

61 ★ LANG, Andrew. Aladdin and the Wonderful Lamp.
      Illustrated by Errol LeCain. Viking, 1981.

Here is the elaborately illustrated tale of the Persian
boy Aladdin, whose chance encounter with a stranger led
to the genie of the ring and the even more powerful
genie of the wonderful lamp. No childhood would be
complete without a sharing of this age-old tale, and this
version captures all the mythic quality of Aladdin's
strange and magical world. Errol LeCain's illustrations
can be studied again and again for their rich detail.

Activities

1) Magic Acrostic (to broaden vocabulary through concept-
related words): Find words to complete the acrostic below. All must be related to magic.

1)M _ _ _ _ _ _ _
    2)A _ _
 _ 3)G _ _ _ _
     4) I _ _
 _ _ 5)C _ _ _ _ _ _ _

1) One who makes magic
2) Magic object
3) Lives in a magic lamp
4) Magic creature
5) Used to evoke a magic spell

2) Select a word from the world of magic tales and
develop your acrostic for others to solve.

62 ★ LASKER, David. The Boy Who Loved Music. Illus-
    trated by Joe Lasker. Viking, 1979.

Karl is a horn-player in the orchestra of Prince
Nicolaus Esterhazy. As fall drags on, the Prince stays
at his summer castle keeping his unhappy musicians
away from their families in Vienna. Pleading for a
return to the city is to no avail. Finally Franz Joseph
Haydn, the director, composes an unusual Farewell
Symphony, which delights the Prince and enables the
musicians to leave. Based on an actual incident, this
book is filled with visual delight and should stimulate
young readers to want to discover the Farewell Symphony for themselves.

Activities

1) Discuss: Can music make you feel different? What
kind of music makes you happy? What happens to you
when you hum? Would you rather hum or whistle?
   Can you find stories about other famous composers?
Is it important to be friends with everyone? Why?
Is it nice for friends to do things together? Why?
What are some fun things that friends can do together?

2) Let the children tell a story to some classical music,
using the music to emphasize and determine events.
Have the children dance to the rhythm.
   Put on a record or play an instrument and ask the
children to draw their own picture of the music.

3) Let the children make their own musical instruments.
They can fill little boxes, shoe-polish tins, or plastic
cups with dried split peas, beans, corn, rice, or anything that makes an interesting sound. They can paint
or decorate the boxes, or, if the plastic cup is transparent, add colored bits of paper in with the sound

makers. Both ends of a string can be inserted in the
shoe-polish tin as it is closed, giving a handle to hold
on to while shaking the instrument.

63 ★ LeTORD, Bijou. Arf, Boo, Click: An Alphabet of
     Sounds. Four Winds, 1981.

This is the first onomatopoetic alphabet--a delightful
collection of words, sounds, and pictures. Expressive
words, like the grrr of a bear, the vroom of an engine,
and the click of a camera, are so often used and rarely
explained. And what better way for children to learn
than to imitate these special sounds and see them in
context with animals, people, plants, and machines.
Bijou LeTord's simple, colorful illustrations match the
sounds, making this a gleeful way to learn the ABCs.

Activities

1) Animal Sounds Crossword:

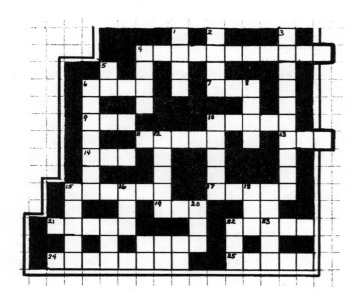

ACROSS | DOWN

4. Snort snort says _____.
6. A cub is a baby _____.
7. Santa's helper.
9. Buzzz says the pesky ___.
10. Gaggle gaggle says the _____.
11. Weapon used in hunting animals: _____.
13. A pigeon says _____.
14. Noah built an _____.
15. _____ says turkey.
17. Grrr says the _____.
19. A kind of deer: _____ buck
21. _____ says squeeak.
22. _____ goes splish splash.
24. Mother _____ gives her baby a shower.
25. Rabbits live in _____.

1. Roar says the _____.
2. A _____ brought Noah an olive branch.
3. The _____ is busy on the tree.
4. Albino animals are ___.
5. A pronoun: _____.
6. Ballooow says the _____.
8. Croak says the old ___.
10. Pig says _____.
12. Author's first name: ___.
16. A _____ gathers pollen.
18. Tiger sound: _____.
20. A snakelike fish: _____.
23. _____ says Whoooo.

2) Try creating your own sounds crossword, perhaps using people sounds or machine sounds.

64 ★ LEWIS, Eils Moorhouse.   The Snug Little House.
     Illustrated by Elise Primavera.   Atheneum, 1981.

Here is a delightful tale that will have children joining in as each of its strange characters is added.   One fine sunny day, a red-velvet chair with loose springs in its seat came down the road.   "Hi!" said a table standing under a nearby tree, "Where are you going?"   "Down the road a piece," answered the chair.   Since the table had a broken leg, it decided to join the chair and off they went.   In their travels they are joined by dishes, silverware, an old bed, and a frayed rug.   They end their travels at the door of a little house and make themselves a home inside.   It takes only the touch of a tiny old woman to make it a snug house indeed, by mending and caring for the discarded objects.   A warm, reassuring cumulative tale.

Activities

1) Discuss: Have you ever helped someone whom you
didn't know?
   What are some simple things that you can do every
day to help people   (e.g., smile, open doors, be happy,
encourage and enjoy someone, tell someone that he or
she is special)?
   Have you ever been to a strange place and felt scared
or alone? Who would you like to see or meet if you
were lost? Why?
   If you could shut your eyes and be anywhere, where
would you be?
   What are some differences between the country and
the city? Who has lived in a city? Who has lived in
the country? (Let the children share the good things
about living in each place.)

2) Let the children make a book to give to a special
friend of theirs. Suggest a different title for each page,
such as:

   a) This is a picture of my friend.
   b) Why I like my friend.
   c) How she helps me.
   d) What I do to make him happy.
   e) How we share together.
   f) Here is a picture of my friend and me sharing.
   g) We like to do these things together....

65 ★ LOBEL, Anita and Arnold. On Market Street. Green-
       willow, 1981.

   Inspired by seventeenth-century French trade engrav-
ings, Anita Lobel has created a stunning alphabet book
in which each of the shopkeepers is composed of his or
her wares. The rhythmic text begins:

   "The merchants down on Market Street
   Were opening their doors.
   I stepped along that Market Street
   I stopped at all the stores."

And what stores there are! Apples (food for the body),
books (food for the mind), clocks, doughnuts, eggs,
flowers--the list goes on, with each seller more elab-

orate than the last.   Children will look at this unusual
ABC book again and again.

Activities

1) Challenge students to select one item that can be
found for sale in the local store or shopping center and
write a definition of that item without naming it.   Defi-
nitions are then read aloud, and each child who guesses
correctly then reads his or her definition.

2) Create a character.   Ask students to collect one type
of scrap material for one week (egg cartons, cloth
scraps, buttons, leaves, old magazines).   When enough
has been gathered, characters can be created from the
material (one type of material to a character).   Each
student can write a prose or poetry description telling
about his or her character's special needs or abilities.

66 ★ LOBEL, Arnold.   Fables.   Harper & Row, 1980.

Here is a collection of original fables, each with a
fresh and unexpected moral.   Children will delight in
tales that picture a pig flying through marshmallow
clouds to a marzipan moon; a wolf who looks suspiciously
like an apple tree; or a bear in a frying-pan hat and
paper-bag boots.   As with many lessons in life, Fables
teaches with laughter.

Activities

1) Discuss the elements of a fable (very short, few
characters, teaches a lesson).   Challenge children to
create fables of their own using these elements.

2) Ask students to search for and combine pictures from
old magazines to show their understanding of the following morals:

   a) "Without a doubt, there is such a thing as too
      much order. "
   b) "At times, a change of routine can be most health-
      ful. "
   c) "It is the high and mighty who have the longest
      distance to fall. "

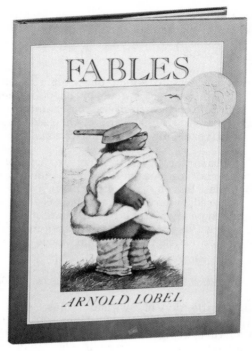

Fables

d) "Even the taking of small risks will add excitement to life."
e) "It is always difficult to pose as something that
one is not."

67 ★ LOBEL, Arnold. Ming Lo Moves the Mountain. Greenwillow, 1982.

How does one move a bothersome mountain? Even
youngest listeners will consider this to be an impossible
task and will delight in Ming Lo's assumption that to
rid himself of the mountain all he has to do is seek the
counsel of the wise man. The wise man suggests pushing a tree against the side of the mountain to move it,
but alas, the tree, not the mountain gives in first. In
turn, Ming Lo follows the wise man's advice to try noise
and gifts to the mountain spirit. Neither works, but on

his final trip to the wise man a workable solution is
found that proves satisfactory to everyone.   The beautiful illustrations enhance both the text and the mood of
the book.

Activities

1) Challenge students to complete the following sentence
in as many ways as they can.   Suggestions can be written on a large chart or on the board as a language-
experience reading lesson for primary grades.

Once this was impossible but now _____
_____ can be done every day.

2) A dictionary of synonyms and a thesaurus give many
words that are related in meaning.   For example, for
the word said one might find:

remarked	advised
ordered	counseled
shouted	complained
demanded	

Retell one part of the story using one or more of the
above words in place of the word said.

Example: The wife demanded that Ming Lo go once
again to the wise man.

68 ★ LORENZ, Lee.   Pinchpenny John.   Prentice-Hall, 1981.

      Suggested by incidents in Chaucer's "The Miller's
Tale," this is the story of a crusty old carpenter named
John, his granddaughter, Allison, and their scheming
boarder, Nicholas, a student of astrology.   Nicholas
plots to steal the old man's gold, concocting an outrage-
ous plan to survive the disastrous flood that he predicts.
But Nicholas had not foreseen the loyalty and love Allison had for her grandfather, and the plan, with her help,
goes amiss in a riotous way!   Lorenz captures the flavor
of the period and the mood of each moment with his
richly detailed, humorous illustrations.

Activities

1) Pinchpenny John is a moral tale in keeping with the

tales of Chaucer's era. Discuss the term moral and
point out the similarities found in moral tales and in
fables. A moral can be defined as a rule for living.
Ask children to write morals of their own--make it a
real challenge by giving them the first letter of each
word.

G_____   I_____   B_____   T_____   T_____

Students may come up with: Giving is better than taking, or Grumbling is bad, talk touchingly!

Try:

R_____   S_____   G_____   N_____   M_____
W_____   I_____   R_____   I_____   S_____

2) Students may enjoy reading about other misers in
literature. One that immediately will come to mind
with middle- and upper-grade students is Scrooge.
This is an ideal time to introduce to these students
Charles and Mary Lamb's Tales from Shakespeare.
Are there misers in any of these tales? Tales can be
related to the class by various students, each stressing
the miser's fate. Also use The Bookfinder, a subject
guide to children's books, to locate other tales of miserliness or selfishness.

69 ★ LOW, Joseph. Mice Twice. Atheneum, 1980.

     A hungry cat invited a mouse to dinner, but mouse
accepted only if she could bring a friend. Mouse's
friend turned out to be a dog, and the cat's plans for
a mouse dinner were quickly dropped. When dog in-
vited cat to dinner the following night, cat decided to
try a little turnabout. Thus continues a series of din-
ners with each guest bigger than the last. Mouse puts
an end to the hilarious proceedings by producing a mystery guest who is small, but mighty!

Activities

1) Little Mouse is constantly confronting a big animal;
thus a natural comparison of opposites can follow. Given
a word written on the board, the children can provide the

opposite.   After a number of pairs are produced, each
child can be assigned to illustrate one pair (including
the written words themselves, of course).   After their
rough drafts are checked for accuracy, the children can
make their finished product on uniform paper and compile the whole into a book.   You, or a class-selected
person, would provide the cover page.   Perhaps a big
elephant peering at a little mouse would be appropriate,
with the title "Our Own Book of Opposites."   Be certain
each page is signed, get the book bound, and let the
class proudly display it for the school.

2) Just so the children don't forget Little Mouse, let
them make a Little Mouse bookmark to keep their places
every day.   Cut felt strips 1" wide and 5" long.   Let
the children clip one end to a point.   Make felt ears
and nose.   Movable eyes are easily glued to the felt.
The whiskers are sewn on with one stitch each under
the nose.   Finally a long yarn tail is glues to the other
end.

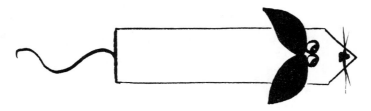

3) Discuss with children what they consider to be important elements in a friend.   Be sure they have noticed
the emotional expressions of surprise, fright, amaze-
ment, etc., evident on the animals' faces in this book.
List the letters of the word friend vertically on the
board, and as a group activity have the students choose
a word that begins with each letter and that they agree
is a characteristic of a friend: Faithful

                                                                    Reliable

                                                                    Interesting

                                                                    Earnest

                                                                    Neighborly

                                                                    Decent

70 ★ LURIE, Alison. Fabulous Beasts. Illustrated by
        Monika Beisner. Farrar, Straus & Giroux, 1981.

        The author and artist have combined efforts to create
        a stunning new collection, Fabulous Beasts. The Veget-
        able Lamb, a lamb that grows on a tree and provides
        fleece far superior to that of real sheep; the Mimick
        Dog, a dog that can imitate the voices and actions of
        other animals; and the Catoblepas, a beast whose head
        is so heavy that it cannot lift it from the ground--these
        are just a few of the unusual creatures portrayed. With
        full-color illustrations by Monika Beisner, the tales de-
        scribe how they look, where they are found, and their
        purpose, providing the perfect guide for these seeking
        high adventure in the exotic and ancient.

        Activities

        1) Create some fabulous beasts of your own using word
        descriptions. For example:

            a) What do you get when you cross a hippopotamus
               with a bull?
            b) What do you get when you cross a monkey with
               a parrot?
            c) What do you get when you cross a lion with an
               alligator?
            d) What do you get when you cross a tiger with a
               rhinoceros?
            e) What do you get when you cross an elephant with
               a crane?
            f) What do you get when you cross a giraffe with a
               crocodile?
            g) What do you get when you cross a leopard with
               an ape?
            h) What do you get when you cross an ostrich with
               a zebra?

        2) Using any media you wish (drawing, clay, collage,
        wire sculpture, etc.), create one of the animals named
        and described above.

71 ★ McCLUNG, Robert M. Sphinx: The Story of a Cater-
        pillar. Newly revised edition. Illustrated by Carol
        Lerner. Morrow, 1981.

        The tale of the familiar caterpillar known as the

tomato hornworm is a classic in the life-cycle form.
The book covers the span of a year the time the insect
takes to grow from an egg to a caterpillar to a pupa to
a big gray moth. The lone survivor of a hatch of four
eggs, Sphinx has many dangerous encounters before he
reaches maturity. A universal story of nature's re-
newal, Sphinx's tale is distinguished by the accuracy
shared by both the author and artist.

Activity

1) A bit of science and language is a natural followup
to this book. The entire life-cycle of the moth can be
illustrated after a discussion of the changes that occur
from stage to the next. An introduction to (or review
of) the days of the week would also be in order. Re-
reading the book will allow the children to sequence the
days orally.

2) A walking caterpillar provides a fun way to incorpor-
ate all the concepts presented. Let the children use a
pattern for the body and the head. Add antennae and
decorate with crayons. A heavy grade of construction
paper works best. Cut holes in the seven scallops (for
the seven days of the week). Let each child insert seven
fingers and watch the caterpillars walk.

72 ★ MANNICHE, Lise.   The Prince Who Knew His Fate.
        Philomel, 1982.

Here is an ancient Egyptian tale translated from hiero-
glyphs, which are reproduced along with the English
translation. This is one of the oldest known fairy tales
in the world. When the prince was born, the seven
Hathor goddesses warned his parents that he would be
killed by a dog, a crocodile, or a snake. His parents
tried to protect him from his harsh fate by keeping him
within a high-walled stone house, but as he grew to
young manhood, the prince tired of this restricted way
of life and decided to seek his fortune in the world.

In a foreign land, hiding his true identity, he won a
contest for the hand of a beautiful princess, only to be
faced by his three fated enemies. Courage, cleverness,
and a bit of magic were needed before he could share
a happy ending with his royal bride. The book provides,
for middle-grade students, an enjoyable experience of a
culture far removed in both time and space.

Activity

   Following a museum visit and/or research on ancient
Egyptian life,

   a) View and discuss: 1) hieroglyphics as Egyptian
      form of communication; and 2) recurring symbols:
      eye, scarab, horus, cobra, cat, ankh.

   b) Divide class into five groups according to a sym-
      bol. Have them find their symbols in a book or
      the museum gallery. The leader then draws each
      group's symbols. Teachers explain the meaning
      behind each symbol and also discuss how one sym-
      bol can express a whole thought or idea.

   c) Pick partners comparable in size. Trace around
      each other on large craft paper.

   d) Fill in body area with pictographs depicting a story
      about where the student's soul, or "ka," went after
      death.

   e) Cut out body shapes and, with symbols and picto-
      graphs on the outside, staple partners' bodies to-
      gether and stuff with paper. Hang these around
      school and write a short story explaining symbols
      depicted on the mummies.

   f) Discuss cartoon-type figures, asking students such
      questions as: Can you tell what's happening by
      looking at the pictures? Is this an effective form
      of communication? Why would people use pictures
      instead of letters to communicate?

   g) Copy dialogue from newspaper cartoons and dis-
      tribute one per child. Have each child draw a
      series of pictures acting out the dialogue.

    h) Students read and decipher each other's cartoon
    pictures.

73 ★ MAYER, Mercer. Ah-Choo! Dial, 1976.

    In this wordless picture book an elephant sneezes at
a bunch of flowers, a mouse, and a shack, blowing them
all down. A policeman scolds the elephant, but the
elephant points to the mouse and the mouse points to the
elephant, each blaming the other. The policeman hand-
cuffs both and takes them to court to talk to the judge--
but the elephant sneezes at the judge, blowing him out
of the building. The judge sends the elephant and mouse
to jail, where the elephant sneezes again, blowing down
part of the jail. And thus the sneeze continues to get
the elephant in and out of troubles that children will find
more humorous than serious!

Activities

1) Do you have a message that you would like to tell
someone?--something that is important to you: a cause,
or a feeling, such as "Don't pollute, give a hoot!" A
good way to tell everyone is with a T-shirt. Have the
students bring in an old or new T-shirt. Using scop
paper, have them design what they would like their T-
shirt to say and draw it actual size. When designs are
ready, use water-base fabric paint. Put in a dryer for
thirty minutes to set the color permanently. When paint
is dry, wash in cold water.

2) Have the students draw or paint what they thought happened to the elephant and hippo after they walked off hand
in hand, or to the mouse and policeman.

74 ★ MAYER, Mercer. Appelard and Liverwurst. Four
        Winds, 1978.

    Appelard was a farmer without a mule. His had been
blown away in a tornado, like the circus and his barn,
which is why the animals slept in the house. One night
they heard a noise in the cellar, and all went down to
see what it was. It was a baby rhinoceros from the
circus. They named him Liverwurst, and Appelard used

Liverwurst to pull the plow and get his farm back in
shape.   People came to watch.   They had a good har-
vest and went to market.   But a rhino in town is a very
different thing from a rhino on the farm!   His destruc-
tive tendencies land him in jail, and from there one adventure leads to another until the heroes finally buy their
very own, very successful circus.

Activities

1) Using the circus theme, students can make up their
faces like clowns.   Some theater groups will come in
and show how it is done with greasepaint.   If the proper
materials can be found, all will enjoy this project.   Be
sure to have students wear old shirts (their parents')
when applying makeup.   If mirrors are scarce, the students can work in groups of two, making up each other.

2) A study of the rhinoceros can take off from this book.
Several statements were made about such characteristics
of the rhinoceros as diet or signaling.   Research results
can be illustrated without words, as in a drawing or
painting of the natural environment, including food, enemies, and so on.   Using bright fluorescent crayons,
draw your picture (leave some paper not drawn) then
take watered-down tempera (black) and brush over picture.   The crayon resists the paint and leaves a black
background.

75 ★ MAYER, Mercer.   Little Monster's Neighborhood.
        Golden, 1978.

Little Monster is telling about his neighborhood.   He
shows us where he lives in relationship to the rest of
the town.   He tells of his best friend and what the two
of them do: secret clubs, shopping, visiting the gas
station, market, and police station; going to church, the
drug store, a Sunday drive; swimming and ice skating.
He tells of the monsters who visit his neighborhood: the
milk monster, paper monster, etc.   He has a babysitter,
even though he doesn't need one, and visits the doctor
(the only human in the book).   Little Monster visits the
library, tells how to check out a book, and on the way
home walks past the haunted house.   That night Little
Monster has a glass of milk and homemade cookies his
mother made--the best.   A delightful addition to studies
on Our Neighborhood in primary grades.

Activities

1) Little Monster has a nice neighborhood. Let's name
some of the places he has to visit in his neighborhood.
List on the board:

house	swimming hole
club house	people
gas station	doctor
market	library
church	haunted house
drug store	streets
farm	park
parade	

Can you name what you have in your neighborhood
that Little Monster doesn't have?

2) Neighborhood Mural: You will need a large sheet of
butcher or brown paper, approximately 15'x4'.   Clear a
space on the floor and have the students draw or paint
a mural of a town.   The teacher should have some idea
of a basic layout, done in pencil, or have the students
talk about it before they start.   Discuss where everything should be placed (depends on age group).   Try and
have the students make many of the above buildings and
more in their mural.   Hang for display.

3) Construction of a Paper Town: Have each student
make a house, church, or one of the above items out
of construction paper and assemble.   (Milk cartons
painted or covered work well.)   Let several students
and the teacher take a table five or six feet long, and
lay a large piece of butcher paper over it to make
streets and parks for the town.   Houses will sit on top.
This brown paper can be colored with paint, crayons,
or magic markers.   Houses can be set, stapled, glued,
or taped on the butcher paper.   Be sure to make some
people to go with the village.   You can spend a longer
amount of time on this project and let the students make
hills (papier mâché or crumbled papers covered with
smooth paper), bridges (cut-out milk cartons), and lakes
(mirrors or aluminum foil).   There are many things you
can make or change it as the year goes on to show how
a town progresses.   Use this to fill in the ten minutes
before lunch or if a student finishes an assignment early.

76 ★ MOERI, Louise. The Unicorn and the Plow. Illus-
      trated by Diane Goode. Dutton, 1982.

      There was once a poor farmer whose crops wouldn't
grow. Every day he went out with his oxen to till the
fields, but every day new weeds sprang up again. Then
one day, when things couldn't get any worse, a miracle
happened. Here is a gentle and engaging fable by the
author of Star Mother's Youngest Child (Houghton
Mifflin, 1975), about a man of unassuming kindness.

Activity

      Making Decisions: Suppose the miracle hadn't hap-
pened? What might the farmer have done to rid his
field of leaves? List your alternatives and the criteria
the farmer must consider. What is his best choice of
action!

Alternatives	Criteria					
3 = yes 2 = maybe 1 = no	will it harm other farm life		will the weeds be gone for good			Total Score
1) Spray with weed- killer						
2) Plow up the field and start over						
3) Sell the farm						
4)						
5)						

77 ★ MYLLER, Rolf. A Very Noisy Day. Atheneum, 1981.

      This book tells about Fred, the dog, who has a day
of disasters--spilling water on the kitchen floor, running across the street and causing an accident, getting
chased by a terrible cat, etc.--that ends with his being

a hero and capturing a bank-robber. The pictures
are of two kinds: small spots of Fred in his various difficulties, and large pictures of words--the
sounds that make Fred's day so noisy. Some of
the sounds are Fred's, and some are made by the
people, animals, and machines that upset Fred or
that Fred upsets. Readers may want to dramatize
the sounds aloud or write a story about sounds
they know.

Activities

1) Vowel sounds can be long (the letter says its name),
short, or silent (not heard at all). Tell whether the
vowel sounds from these words in A Very Noisy Day
are long, short, or silent.

_____ day	_____ kitchen	_____ chase
_____ Fred	_____ run	_____ cat
_____ dog	_____ street	_____ bank
_____ water	_____ accident	_____ rob

2) Write a new story about Fred titled A Very Quiet
Day. What would cause Fred to have a quiet day?
How will your readers know it is a quiet day? What
quiet words will you use? What kinds of quiet things
will Fred do on this day? Will Fred enjoy his quiet
day or does he want the day to change?

78 ★ NOBLE, Trinka Hakes. The Day Jimmy's Boa Ate the
     Wash. Illustrated by Steven Kellogg. Dial, 1980.

In this study in reversibility a class plans a trip to
a farm, but as one incident leads to another the entire
farm is out of control! The cow cries, the farmer
crashes into the haystack with his tractor, the pigs get
on the bus and eat the lunches, the children threw corn
because they ran out of eggs to throw and, of course,
the boa constrictor ate the wash. Sound confusing? It
really becomes quite a logical series of events when
told by one young hero of the tale.

Activities

1) Divide the class into groups of five or six. Allow

each group five minutes to develop its own chain-of-events story. If possible, place at least one child in each group who likes to sketch. As each group tells its story, one child from the group sketches the events across the blackboard. Remind the groups that the final event must lead to a retelling of the story.

2) Mix and match magazine illustrations or comic-strip frames to create a wordless chain-of-events story for others to interpret.

79 ★ OAKLEY, Graham. Magical Changes. Atheneum, 1979.

Here children can make countless pairings and magical changes of the illustrations simply by turning the half-page of the book. Gentlemen carrying umbrellas become gentlemen supporting tree trunks alive with spider webs, or carrying a wedding cake. Swan bodies hold up bridges, become candles, or turn into the bottom of the famous Trojan Horse. The combinations are endless and will give hours of observant pleasure to the young viewer.

Activities

1) Discuss: Why is it important to do things differently? Can you think of any habits that you have--something that you just do over and over again without thinking? How could you do that in a fresh, new way? Why is it important to be creative?

2) Have the children write a poem, beginning each line with:

I feel creative when I _____.
Life is more interesting when I _____.

Now have them write a poem, using the same ideas but beginning each line differently.

80 ★ PANEK, Dennis. Detective Whoo. Bradbury, 1981.

Never a moment's peace for Detective Whoo. Eerie night noises disturb his quiet; and he's off to investigate a new case. Out of the blackness the yellow of his flashlight beam isolates strange phenomena: dragons and ghosts, monster footprints, terrifying traps, and man-eaters. But at last dawn comes and the mysterious terrors of the night are revealed--horses' muzzles that looked like dragons, a pouncing tiger on a poster, a clown closeup that appeared to be a ghost. And Detective Whoo has solved his scariest case ever: the circus has come to town!

Activities

1) Detective Whoo proves that things are not always what they seem! Compare this book with Ellen Raskin's Spectacles (Atheneum, 1968), about a little girl who refused to wear glasses; when she finally was persuaded to put on spectacles, she discovered that the world was a very different place than she had imagined.
    Also introduce Arnold Lobel's book The Ice Cream Cone Coot and Other Rare Birds (Four Winds, 1971), which uses the basic line of an object (in this case, familiar household objects) as the starting point for elaboration.

2) What familiar item can each student take to elaborate on? A pencil can be a good choice. A pencil and boxes of paper or cloth scraps allow students the freedom to experiment. They can add to the pencil, change its shape or color, or combine it with other objects. When their new creations are finished, each student must give the name of his or her object and tell what it is used for. Each object can serve as a starting point for a short story or poem telling about its unique qualities.

81 ★ PARENTEAU, Shirley. I'll Bet You Thought I Was Lost.
    Illustrated by Lorna Tomei. Lothrop, Lee & Shepard, 1981.

    Sandy goes to the supermarket with his dad, when suddenly his father disappears. Suddenly, as well, the aisles look longer, the stacks higher, and the shopping carts and legs familiar. On his father's trail, Sandy explores the supermarket with a new, detective eye, finding clues throughout to remind him of home. A contemporary adventure that will ring bells with any child who has ever taken a wrong turn.

Activities

1) Let the children make a picture of a store, with
themselves and their friends hidden in it, as part of
the stock.   For example:

   --skinny Steve as a toothpaste tube
   --freckled Francis as a bolt of dotted swiss
   --beaming Bob as a banana
   --mini Margie as a clothespin.

2) Make silhouette pictures of the children.   Have them
sit in front of a bright light.   Tape a piece of paper
onto the wall where their shadow falls.   Trace their
shadow on the paper.   Notice the different shapes of
the heads and hair.

82 ★ PARKER, Nancy Winslow. Cooper: The McNallys'
    Big Black Dog. Dodd, Mead, 1981.

How can you sell a dog who has absolutely no talents?
Cooper can't seem to do anything right.   He can't qualify
as a guard dog, a show dog, or a hunting dog, so father
decides to sell him.   Yet in the end Cooper saves the
day with a very unique talent no one guessed he had!

Activities

1) After enjoying the antics of Cooper, children should
stretch their imaginations in composing For Sale ads
for other animals not generally thought of as pets.   For
example, how many uses might one have for a tarantula?
An octopus?   A hippopotamus?

2) Write a short, "pretend" Pet Care booklet explaining
to the new owner how to care for the unusual pet.   You
may want to include such items as what to feed your
pet, where to obtain food, how to house and exercise
your pet, and what to do for your pet should it become
ill.

83 ★ PATERSON, Katherine, translator. The Crane Wife,
    by Sumiko Yagawa.   Illustrated by Suekichi Akaba.
    Morrow, 1981.

A poor farmer marries a lovely stranger not long

Cooper: The McNallys' Big Black Dog

after he has rescued a wounded crane from death. Content with his new happiness at first, the young man obeys his wife's request that he not watch as she weaves and cooks. But eventually, listening to bad advice and growing greedy, he breaks his promise and in doing so forfeits his happiness. He loses his paradise and his crane wife returns to her own. In this beautifully illustrated book the artist uses open spaces and sparely drawn figures to invite viewers to complete the picture with their own imagination.

Activities

1) Children can think about the contrast in lifestyles of people they know, or contrast their own lifestyle with that of a friend or family member. For example, following the four- or five-line format of the answers given in the book, a child can answer the questions "What do I do for fun?" and "What does my grandmother do for fun?" The students' original short verses should be read to the class.

2) Before presenting this book to primary children, the teacher may want to borrow a number of books on children

The Crane Wife (illustration © 1981 by Suekichi Akaba)

of other lands from the library for the classroom reading table. After allowing a day or two for browsing,
read The Crane Wife. Ask the children to find similarities and differences in the way people from different
countries do the same thing--eating, sleeping, etc.

84 ★ PEPPE, Rodney. The Mice Who Lived in a Shoe.
        Lothrop, Lee & Shepard, 1981.

    Every day, life was getting worse for the family of
mice who lived in an old shoe. They had little protection from nasty weather, and almost none at all from

the neighborhood cat when he stuck his paw and tried
to grab them for his supper. So they decided to build
a dream house right out of what they had. And with
all the family working together, the house began to grow.
Everyone contributed both work and ideas, from drawing
the plans to building the finished product. Here is a
delightful introduction to the critical thinking skill of
planning. First the mice brainstorm for ideas. Then
ideas are examined and choices are made to include the
best in the house plans. Tools and materials are considered, as well as problems that might be encountered.
As the dreamhouse nears completion, the mice discover
that planning has paid off, for:

> "When it rained they kept dry.
> When it snowed they kept warm.
> When the sun shone they kept cool.
> When the wind blew they stayed safe inside.
> But the best thing of all was when the cat came to
> put his paw into the shoe to stretch out his claws ...
> he couldn't!"

Activities

1) Allow the children to plan a classroom reading corner.
Ask for input from all class members. Assign one or
two students to design the corner and to present the plans
to the class for approval or revision.

2) Consider alternatives to a reading corner. Consider
a reading "cave" in which individual children can read.
This can consist of a card table covered with a blanket,
or a large box, such as a refrigerator carton.

85 ★ PINKWATER, Daniel.   Tooth-Gnasher Superflash.   Four
     Winds, 1981.

   Mr. Sandy has lots of shiny new cars to sell, but the
five little Popsnorkles have their hearts set on the Tooth-
Gnasher Superflash. "It's a lovely shade of blue, " adds
Mrs. Popsnorkle as Mr. Popsnorkle gets behind the
wheel for a test drive.
   When he pushed a button on the dashboard, Tooth-
Gnasher Superflash takes off. Other automobiles may
have the names of animals, but this car turns into them!
It becomes a dinosaur running along the road, then be-

comes an elephant and a turtle. When the car transforms itself into an airborne chicken, Mr. Popsnorkle
heads back to the car lot, determined to buy it.
    "Yaay," say the five little Popsnorkles. "We love
our new car!" Powered by Pinkwater, Tooth-Gnasher
Superflash is an incredible joy ride, with a running
start and a flying finish.

Activities

1) After students have enjoyed their trip in the Tooth-
Gnasher Superflash, share another memorable motor-
car trip with them. Read aloud the chapter in Wind in
the Willows where Toad discovers the motor car, or
read aloud the following paragraph:
    "There you are!" cried Toad. "There's the real life
for you embodied in that little cart. The open road, the
dusty highway, the heath, the common, the hedgerows,
the rolling downs! Camps, villages, towns, cities!
Here today, up and off to somewhere else tomorrow.
Travel, change, interest, excitement! The whole world
before you and a horizon that's always changing!"
    These are the words of Toad from Wind in the Wil-
lows when he falls in love with a motor car. It's fun
to look at a paragraph of prose and spot the key words,
which can be rearranged to create a poem.

        A TRAVELING CART
        AN EAGER TOAD
        TRAVELING DOWN THE OPEN ROAD
        HIGHWAYS, COMMONS, ROLLING DOWNS
        TOWNS AND CITIES, LAUGHING CLOWNS
        HERE TODAY AND GONE TOMORROW,
        THE TRAVELER'S LIFE IS JOY, NOT SORROW

2) Here's another paragraph from the book. Try creating your own poem from it. Toad describes his car:
    "Glorious, stirring sight, the poetry of motion! The
REAL way to travel. The ONLY way to travel. Villages
skipped, towns and cities jumped, always somebody else's
horizon! What a flowery track lies spread before me.
What dust clouds shall spring up behind me as I speed
on my reckless way. That swan! That sunbeam! That
Thunderbolt! O Bless! O my! O my!"

86 ★ POMERANTZ, Charlotte. If I Had a Paka: Poems in

Eleven Languages.   Illustrated by Nancy Tafuri.
Greenwillow, 1982.

Children will discover that by reading or hearing the
poems in this book they can understand Serbo-Croatian,
Swahili, Vietnamese, and other languages they never
thought they knew. Rather than an English/other-language
translation, the poems use both languages, and children
gain meaning of unfamiliar words and phrases from the
context of each poem as well as from the illustrations.
For example, the first poem says:

> "If I had a paka
> meow, meow,
> meow, meow
> I would want a mm-bwa
> Bow wow wow wow."

Even the youngest listener is able to identify word
meanings through association with familiar words and
phrases.

Activities

1) Using If I Had a Paka as a model, encourage children
to write their own poems, integrating words from another
language.   Survey the class to see if another language
might be spoken at home; or ask a student from another
land to share several nouns and their meaning from his
or her language.   List the words on the board and pro-
nounce them with the children before the writing begins.

2) Illustrate a foreign word: Using the technique of word
illustration (for example, the word Long might be written
all the way across the paper), ask students to show the
meaning of a foreign word from one of the poems.   Example:

> EMPAT
>
> EMPAT
>   means   FOUR
> EMPAT
>
> EMPAT

87 ★ QUACKENBUSH, Robert.   Animal Cracks.   Lothrop,
Lee & Shepard, 1975.

Robert Quackenbush has made up humorous fables to
account for seven old familiar sayings about animals,
such as "His bark is worse than his bite." He introduces animal characters that are met again in later
books, such as Detective Mole (Lothrop, Lee and
Shepard, 1976). He seems to enjoy his characters,
and this adds to the fun one feels in reading the book.

Activities

1) Discuss what each of the expressions really means.
See if the children can give an everyday example for
each meaning.
    Use a book like Hog on Ice (Warner Paperback Library,
1973), or Heavens to Betsy (Warner Paperback Library,
1972), both by Charles Funk, to find the origin of many
sayings.
    Explain that these stories are not really fables, al-
though they follow somewhat the same pattern, that of
using animal characters (as fables often do) and using
a story to explain some happening or moral. Read and
discuss some of Aesop's Fables.

2) Give each child or group of children an old saying.
Ask them to draw a picture to illustrate the saying
literally.
    Have each child choose one of the sentences to com-
plete and illustrate:

I feel light as a _____ .

It was as dark as _____ .

She's mean as _____ .

He's big as _____ .

My hands are cold as _____ .

88 ★ QUACKENBUSH, Robert.   Clementine: Music!   Pictures!
        How to Pan for Gold!   Lippincott, 1974.

    Robert Quackenbush uses the well-known folksong of
the Gold Rush days as the plot and setting for an old-
time melodrama.   The story is told by using selected
verses and inserting pictures and "asides" as might be
used in a performance.   The book includes the music
and also information on hunting for gold.

Activities

1) This song came from the Gold Rush era of 1849 and is therefore a natural springboard to a discussion of the Gold Rush. Let the children tell what they know about the Gold Rush. Listen carefully to what they contribute, and clear up misconceptions they may have gained from television stories. Bring out how the Gold Rush contributed to the settlement of the lands in the West.

Discuss problems caused by so many people arriving in an area so quickly. What were some of the difficulties people had? What kinds of shortages were there? What were some other ways of earning a living in a "boom town" besides finding gold?

What kind of a "find" might cause a "rush" today? Would the problems be the same? Have students brainstorm various causes.

2) Why don't we hear of gold rushes today? Might we have another gold rush?

This book also leads naturally into a discussion of melodrama. What is it? Where have students seen melodrama? What types of characters are in a melodrama? What kind of an ending did most melodramas have?

Suggest that the students dramatize the story. A simple device is to use a bow to denote the characters. The bow is placed in the hair for the heroine, under the chin for the hero and above the lips as a mustache for the villain. A small group at the side can be the chorus and either sing a refrain or do a choral reading.

3) Treasure Hunt: Look in your library for fiction books by the following authors. Find and list a book by each one with either GOLDEN, SILVER, or TREASURE in the title.

Bulla, Clyde	(Ghost Town Treasure)
Corbin, William	(The Golden Mare)
O'Dell, Scott	(The Treasure of Topo-el-Bampo)
Miller, Edna	(Mousekin's Golden House)
Clymer, Eleanor	(Santiago's Silver Mine)
Orton, Helen	(The Treasure in the Little Trunk)
Yashima, Taro	(The Golden Footprints)

Cooper, Susan   (Silver on the Tree)

Stevenson, Robert L.   (Treasure Island)

Whitney, Phyllis   (The Mystery of the Golden Horn)

Ward, Lynd   (The Silver Pony)

Cunningham, Julia   (The Treasure Is the Rose)

(Note to teachers: The same information can be found
in the card catalog if the children think of it.   Don't
suggest it, but don't discourage it if they come up with
the idea.   Teachers will need to check to see if these
books are in the library.   If not, substitutions can be
made.)

89 ★ QUACKENBUSH, Robert. Detective Mole. Lothrop,
    Lee & Shepard, 1976.

As soon as Maynard Mole finished his studies at the
Detective School, he set up an office and was ready to
go to work.   In this book he solves five mini-mysteries
for the animals that were introduced to readers in the
author's book Animal Cracks (see entry 87).

Activities

1) What does Detective Mole have that lets us know he
is a detective?   Why are these items symbols of a detective?   Why does Detective Mole wear sun glasses?
Why is this amusing?   Can you think of any other job
that would be an unlikely job for a mole to have?   What
jobs would be unlikely ones for some other animals?
    Pretend that you are one of the chicks in the first
mystery.   What would you have said to your parents
when you were pretending to be a ghost?

2) Write a factual report on moles.   Use the encyclopedia or a science book.
    Hide something in the room and list clues that will
lead to where it is hidden.

3) Play the Hidden Word Game: Circle the letter under
Yes or No.   The answer will be the solution to the final
mystery in Detective Mole.   Yes   No

a) A mole is an animal that usually
   lives underground.   P   R

	Yes	No
b) Detective Mole always wears overshoes.	B	A
c) Detective Mole ends each case with "I'll check it out."	C	N
d) Mr. Cat forgot to pay the water bill.	C	N
e) Miss Field Mouse couldn't find her bottle caps.	S	R
f) Pack rats "borrow" shiny objects.	A	B
g) The animals were happy to receive their bills.	S	T

90 ★ QUACKENBUSH, Robert.   Mr. Snow Bunting's Secret.
    Lothrop, Lee & Shepard, 1978.

    In this charming easy-to-read book the author shares
his grandmother's secret of how to make bows for pack-
ages.   Suspense is kept high as Mr. Dog tries to unravel
the mystery of Mr. Snow Bunting's successful package-
wrapping business.

Activity

1) Mr. Dog was jealous of Mr. Snow Bunting's successful business and the praise he received from others.
Help children trace the way Mr. Dog's feelings led him
from jealousy to suspicion and mistrust and finally to
false accusations.   What was Mr. Snow Bunting's reac-
tion?   Tell about a time you have been aware of bad
feelings leading to other bad feelings.   What did you do
about it?   What are different ways you can respond when
you are falsely accused?   Discuss the saying "Two wrongs
don't make a right."   What might have happened if Mr.
Snow Bunting had responded to Mr. Dog in the wrong way?

2) Children will want to try out the bow-making secret.
Let each of them make a bow-maker.   Have the children
bring pieces of ribbon from home to practice on.   A
package-wrapping center may be set up and children can
wrap small boxes to be used later for room decorations.
    Play a guessing game with wrapped boxes.   Bring in
a box.   Tell children to imagine that something very
nice is in the box.   Let them share their thoughts of
what very nice thing might be in the box.   It is not

necessary to be concerned about the size of their "wish"
fitting in the box. Encourage them to let their imagination and wishes have free rein.

91 ★ QUACKENBUSH, Robert.   Pete Pack Rat.   Lothrop,
      Lee & Shepard, 1976.

      Pete Pack Rat was first met in the book Detective
Mole (see entry 89). Now he is back home in Pebble
Junction. This is a hilarious tale of adventure in the
Old West, as the hero heads for a showdown with Giz-
zard Coyote at high noon--a slapstick sagebrush saga.

Activities

1) Pack rats like to pick up shiny objects. How many
shiny things can you think of that a pack rat might pick
up? Do you know of other animals that take shiny things?
      What did you learn about pack rats in this story?
What does it mean when some person is referred to as
a pack rat?
      Summer and Winter Jack Rabbit have a very confus-
ing way of explaining how to tell them apart. Do you
know any twins? How do you tell them apart?
      Read other books to learn about the desert area, such
as True Book of Deserts (Childrens Press, 1972). Find
out about different kinds of cactus.

2) Research to find out all you can about pack rats,
gophers, coyotes, and jackrabbits. You may want to
make a booklet of small desert animals.
      A cactus house would feel very prickly. Make a col-
lection of things that feel prickly. Think of how other
things feel. Start new categories to add to your collection.
      Write a newspaper headline and article about Pete
Pack Rat and his fight with Gizzard Coyote.

92 ★ QUACKENBUSH, Robert.   Pop! Goes the Weasel and
      Yankee Doodle: New York City in 1776 and Today.
      Lippincott, 1976.

      "Pop! Goes the Weasel" was an old favorite song for
which people added new verses to satirize events of the
time. Robert Quackenbush has written new verses as

they might have been used when the British invaded New
York at the time of the American Revolution to tell the
story of the British occupation and the trials and heroism
of the Americans. He continues the story with verses
from "Yankee Doodle." Quackenbush's illustrations show
how New York looked two hundred years ago and how it
looks today. Included at the end are words and music
to both songs and a 1776 tour map of New York City.

Activities

1) The book shows scenes of New York City two hundred
years ago and as it looks today. Talk about how places
in local areas have changed in recent years. How do
you think it looked two hundred years ago? How do you
think the area will look two hundred years in the future?

2) The British sang "Yankee Doodle" to make fun of the
Americans, but the colonists enjoyed the humor of it and
adopted it as their own. Can you think of a time when
you have turned an insult into something funny? How do
you feel when someone makes fun of you? What are
some ways to respond?

3) "Pop goes the weasel" was an old expression with a
special meaning. "Pop" meant to pawn and "weasel"
was a hatmaker's tool, so it meant to pawn one's tools
of trade when times were hard. Why do you suppose
times were hard for the colonists before the American
Revolution?
    How many things can you think of, besides hats, that
were made by hand in those days, rather than in fac-
tories or by machine?

93 ★ QUACKENBUSH, Robert. Take Me Out to the Airfield!
How the Wright Brothers Invented the Airplane. Parents' Magazine, 1976.

    Starting with a poem sung to the tune of "Take Me
Out to the Ball Game," this book uses words and pictures to tell about the invention of the airplane. Additional cartoon-like pictures and comments give more
facts and inject some humor. The book tells how the
Wright boys became interested in flying, what they did
about it, and how they finally invented the airplane. At
the end of the book, directions are given for building a

model of the Wright Flyer, and there is a short section explaining how an airplane flies.

Activities

1) What kind of thing would you like to invent or to see
invented? Tell why you think the invention would be
useful.
    Discuss with your parents or grandparents how inven-
tions have changed the way of life since they were children. Tell about what you have learned.
    The Wright Brothers didn't give up when things went
wrong, even though they were discouraged. This is
called perseverance. Can you think of other famous
people or book characters who persevered? Tell about
yourself or someone you know who did not give up when
things went wrong.

2) Have children pretend to be a newsperson watching
the Wright Brothers' first flight. Write a headline and
newspaper article. Or pretend to be a radio or TV an-
nouncer and give an eyewitness report.
    Make a model flyer from the picture in the book.
Bring in other model planes and have a display. Perhaps they could be put in chronological order.
    Read about some other inventors. Have a parade of
inventors and their inventions.

94 ★ RUSSELL, Sandra. A Farmer's Dozen. Harper & Row,
       1982.

    Here is a delightful introduction to numbers and seria-
tion for young children. In bold, bright colors the
author-artist shows:

        "A farmer working in the sun
        Was all alone, the only one.
        Then one day he said 'I do. '
        He'd found a wife and they were two. "

A spotted cow, a dappled horse, a plump red hen--the
farmer welcomes them one by one until his yard is over-
flowing with a dozen whimsical creatures. Children will
delight in the arrival of each small creature to the farmland scene.

Activities

1) To allow children practice in verbal description, list
on the board the names of each animal in the story.
Ask each child to select one animal and not to reveal
his or her choice. Allow time for the children to think
of ways to describe the animal chosen. As each animal
is orally described, the child who first correctly identi-
fies the animal will be next to give his or her description.

2) To promote reversibility of thought, have students
recount the animals and people in the story in reverse
order. What other farm animals could be added to
bring the number to fifteen? Twenty?

95 ★ SAUNDERS, Susan. A Sniff in Time. Illustrated by
     Michael Mariano. Atheneum, 1982.

To James, every day on the farm was just like every
other day--that is, until the day a scruffy old wizard
came and demanded dinner. James had little to offer--
only some turnips--for which the wizard was not really
grateful. In return he gave James just the ability to
sniff into the future. The result was a disaster. James
smelled spring in the winter and planted too soon. He
smelled a storm on a clear day and shut the cows into
the barn. He smelled smoke when there was no fire
and made everyone angry. Finally his mother sent him
off to find the wizard and have the spell lifted. But instead James found a king for whom someone who could
smell into the future was invaluable, and James's ability
took on a whole new aspect.

Activities

1) What's That Smell? Students should research through
old magazines to locate pictures of people or animals
who appear to be reacting to some kind of smell. Urge
students to look only at the face and to cut out only the
person or animal without any background. Each student
should write what he thinks the person is smelling and
why. Pictures can be exchanged and ideas written about
the second picture. Students should compare their responses to the same picture. Do we all see the same
thing when we look at the same picture?

2) Suppose that James had been given one of the following abilities instead of the ability to sniff into the future:

   The ability to see into the future
   The ability to hear words said in the future
   The ability to touch an object and to tell what will
      happen to it in the future

   How would the story change? Either use this activity
as a class exercise in fluency and flexibility of thought
or suggest that individual students select the one ability
that most appeals and write an elaboration of A Sniff in
Time.   New stories might be titled "A Glance in Time,"
"A Word in Time, " or "A Touch in Time. "

96 ★ SEVERO, Emoke de Papp.   The Good-Hearted Youngest
         Brother.   Illustrated by Diane Goode.   Bradbury,
         1981.

   What a marvelous feast of every kind of good food
and drink for three hungry brothers! And it appeared
to come from nowhere until the boys spied a little man
(a handspan tall) and heard his yells of "Hey, Hey."
Only the youngest had the wit to say, "We thank you for
the good supper. " And just in time, too.   For if he
had not spoken, they might never have heard the riddle
of the three enchanted princesses, and all would have
been turned to stone.   But because the youngest brother
was good-hearted, he was able to solve the riddle, break
the spell upon the beautiful princesses, and bring an entire countryside to life.

Activities

1) Here is the classic tale of the looked-down-upon
youngest brother who saves the day! In comparing this
tale with Aardema's Riddle of the Drum (Four Winds,
1979) or Shulevitz's classic Russian tale The Fool of the
World and the Flying Ship (Farrar, 1968), many similarities will be seen although the settings are very different.   Challenge children to visit the fairy-tale section
of the library and look for other "younger-brother" tales.

2) Older children are often amazed that very similar
tales have become a part of the culture of people who
live very different lives.   Below are a number of the

basic types of tales.   How many students can name or
find at least one example of each:

a) cumulative tales
b) romances
c) transformations
d) simpletons
e) beast tales
f) talking-animal tales

g) magic objects
h) enchantments
i) many trials and tasks
j) unselfish younger daughter
k) witches and/or wizards
l) pourquoi stories

97 ★ SHANNON, George.   Dance Away.   Illustrated by José
Aruego and Ariane Dewey.   Greenwillow, 1982.

Here is a delightful problem-solving tale for the very
young.   Rabbit loved to dance, morning, noon, and night,
and he made his friends dance with him.   Soon they'd
had enough and began to avoid him.   One day Fox was
up to his usual tricks and had captured all of Rabbit's
friends, planning to eat them for his dinner.   And then
along came Rabbit.   How his dancing outfoxed the Fox
makes a lovely and amusing tale.

Activities

1) Role-Play: This is a perfect vehicle for role play.
Assign the parts of Rabbit, Rabbit's friends, and the Fox.
As the teacher reads the tale aloud, children act out the
parts.   Be sure that the "actors" practice the dance
step first!   "Left two three kick, right two three kick,
left skip, turn around."

2) Problem-Solving: While the book may seem simple,
it is really a rather involved exercise in problem-solving.
Examining the text from the author's point of view, share
the book with older students to the point where Rabbit
meets Fox, who has captured all of Rabbit's friends.
Brainstorm for solutions to rabbit's problem:

a) State the factors leading to the problem.
b) State the problem.
c) Brainstorm for possible solutions (alternatives).
d) State what the solution must accomplish (criteria).
e) Examine each alternative in light of established
   criteria.
f) Select the best solution.
g) Finish reading the story.   Compare student solutions with that decided upon by the author.

98 ★ SHANNON, George. Lizard's Song. Illustrated by José
     Aruego and Ariane Dewey. Greenwillow, 1981.

     A delightful book for the very young about a Bear
who wants to learn Lizard's song but can't until he discovers the secret of making a song your very own!
Bold, bright art and repetition of phrases will make
this a favorite with primary children.

Activity

     Reverse the Verse: Lizard has a song. It goes like
this:

          "Zoli zoli zoli - - - zoli zoli zoli
          Rock is my home, what is your home?
          Zoli zoli zoli - - - zoli zoli zoli. "

     Each of these animals want to sing Lizard's song,
but they don't have a rock for a home. Name the home
for each animal given so that they can sing Lizard's
song and put their own home in the verse:

Animal	Animal's Home
a) lizard	rock
b) bear	den
c) goldfish	
d) spider	
e) fox	
f) canary	
g) camel	
h) mole	
i) cow	
j) octopus	
k) duck	
l) bee	

     Now sing Lizard's song. Use another animal's home
and see if some of your friends can guess which animal you
are.

99 ★ SHANNON, George.   The Piney Woods Peddler.   Illus-
      trated by Nancy Tafuri.   Greenwillow, 1981.

> "With a wing wang waddle
> And a great big straddle
> And a Jack-fair-faddle
> It's a long way from home...."

So sang the Piney Woods peddler as he traveled about,
looking for a shiny silver dollar for his dear darling
daughter.   Here is a swapping tale in the truest folk
tradition--and a perfect introduction to making choices!

Activities

1) Trading involves making choices.   Even the youngest
students are faced with choices and can understand the
economic term "opportunity cost."   The term indicates
that for every choice we make there is the cost of another choice not made.   It is important to consider the
opportunity cost by weighing the advantages and disadvantages of a choice.   Ask students to name two things
that they would like to have or do if, for example, they
were to have such a magic wish.   Make two columns
on each side of a paper.   List one item on the front
of the paper and one on the back.   Then ask students
to list all the advantages and disadvantages of each
choice.   Encourage balancing the pros and cons.   Compare the data for the two choices.   Which seems the
better choice?

2) Ask your school librarian to collect books on your
grade level that deal with choices.   If you do not have
a librarian, check with your public library for The
Bookfinder, an extensive subject guide to children's
books, and select those listed under choices.   When
students have had time to read several of the books,
talk with them about characters who had choices to
make.   Do your young readers agree or disagree with
the characters' choices?

100 ★ SHARMAT, Marjorie Weinman.   Gila Monsters Will
        Meet You at the Airport.   Illustrated by Byron
        Barton.   Macmillan, 1980.

Tears about new experiences often arise from pre-

conceived ideas rather than real knowledge. Here are
the anxieties of two children, one who is moving West,
where people "chase buffalos" and "there's cactus
everywhere you look, " and the other, who is moving
East, where the streets "are full of gangsters" and
spring and summer only last five minutes. Here is
a most perceptive picture book that will help children
everywhere to laugh at their own fears about facing
the unknown.

Activities

1) Discuss: Have you ever had a friend who went far
away?   How might you stay close friends even though
you don't see each other?
      Can you have a friend who lives differently than
you do   (e. g. , casual-formal, city-country, wealthy-
poor)?
      Why is it that some people are scared to make
friends with someone different from themselves?   What
is good about having a friend who is different from
ourselves?

2) Choose one state or country where you have never
been.   Make a list of all the things you think you know
about the place you choose.   Ask your librarian to help
you find a recent book about the place.   Read the book.
Put a star by those items on your list that were true
and an x by those items that were not true.   How accurate were you?

101 ★ SHARMAT, Marjorie Weinman.   Lucretia the Unbearable.
        Illustrated by Janet Stevens.   Holiday House, 1981.

      Lucretia Bear has everything in the world wrong
with her, or so she thinks.   She feels worse when
Hunkly Lion tells her there's a wart on her nose or
when she sniffs the sickly smell of paint or when she
thinks she's losing her memory.   Lucretia shares her
worries and complaints with everybody, and her friends
soon get tired of listening to her.   Finally Lucretia
learns that being sick and "thinking" she's sick are
two different things.

Activities

1) Older students will enjoy a discussion of "human

habits that bug" and have fun guessing the reasons for
the odd or annoying habits of others--with a little self-
analysis of their own habits that may "bug" other people. Each student can keep a self-analysis chart for
one week listing one or more habits he or she would
like to break. Points can be self-scored for each success during the week with a followup discussion on why
bad habits are difficult to break and good habits are
sometimes difficult to acquire.

2) Primary students can illustrate one habit they have
that their family likes and one habit that is not so popular at home. Bring into the discussion of the illustrations the point that habits can change and ask students
to cite examples of things they used to do that they no
longer do.

102 ★ SHARMAT, Marjorie Weinman. Twitchell the Wishful.
       Illustrated by Janet Stevens. Holiday House, 1981.

This well-known author-illustrator team have created
another memorable character, Twitchell, who wants
everything his friends have. He admires Claudette's
fireplace, Jacqueline's shoes, Granville's violin, and
Thackery's table. One day Twitchell gets everything
he thinks he wants. Then with the help of his friend
Dawson, Twitchell discovers that he is happiest with
his own things. A delightful book for sharing and discussion with primary children!

Activities

1) Discuss: Do you ever imitate other people? Why?
When and why might it not be so much fun?
    Is it important that we always be ourselves and not
copy or imitate others? Why or why not?
    If you could say something that everyone all over
the world could hear, what would it be?
    Is it always wrong to want something someone else has?

2) In this tale the author explores "the ideas of personal
responsibility and of people discovering in themselves
resources they never suspected." The story is a perfect springboard for discussion of this theme. Discussion should also lead to positive action. What personal
responsibility can I assume to make my school, home,
and/or community a better place to live and work?

103 ★ SHECTER, Ben. Sparrow Song. Harper & Row, 1981.

    As the wrecking crew's hammers, crowbars, and saws begin to tear the old house apart, Sparrow sings of all the good years the house has sheltered. The house is empty now, stripped of most of its life. But Sparrow is not alone. A boy is there, too, listening and watching. And as Sparrow sings, the boy collects bits and pieces of old wood and memories to build a new house and a new home for the small bird.

Activities

1) Discuss the following questions:

    a) What is the difference between a house and a home?
    b) What makes a home a place you want to be?
    c) How many ways can you make your home a more pleasant place to be for everyone who lives there?
    d) What if you arrived home after school and found an empty space where your house or apartment or trailer usually stands. What would you do?
    e) If you were a designer of houses, what would you add that is not usually found in houses today?

2) Where Would You Look? You are a famous naturalist. You have been commissioned by the National Committee for the Preservation of Birds to find and paint each of the following birds. After doing a bit of research, tell where you would be most likely to find the following birds if the month of the year were July.

Name	State	Habitat (ground, tree, etc.)
Robin		
Sparrow		
Blue Jay		
Junko		
Red-Headed Woodpecker		
Nuthatch		
Sea Gull		
Starling		
Pigeon		
Red-Winged Blackbird		

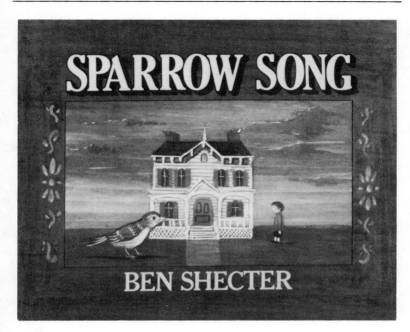

Sparrow Song

Sparrow Song

104 ★ SLATE, Joseph. The Star Rocker. Illustrated by
        Dirk Zimmer. Harper & Row, 1982.

It is a cool September night. The hush of sundown
is broken by the uneasy rustling of the animals that
make their homes around the pond. Old Cassie, too,
lives by the pond, lives on the pond, on a cabin raft.
She understands how the night sounds can startle little
creatures. But Cassie knows how to quiet them down,
how to lull them to sleep with her gentle words and
her gentle rocking. In beautifully descriptive language
the author reveals the small forest creatures and their
natural setting and creates a mood of calm and peace.

Activities

1) Old Cassie explains the following forest sounds to
the small creatures. What other explanations for these
sounds might the children give?

    a) Rustling_____
    b) Creaking_____
    c) Heaving_____
    d) Scraping_____
    e) Slapping_____
    f) Blowing_____

2) Cassiopeia, the star rocker, is appropriately named.
Explain the word constellation. Ask students to find
out more about the constellations from books in the
school library (Dewey Number 523), noting especially
how the constellations were named.

105 ★ STUBBS, Joanna.   Weather Witch.   André Deutsch/
       Dutton, 1981.

       Mr. Mulally would have been happy digging in his
garden if it hadn't been for the rain.   Why wouldn't
it stop?   Then the sad weather witch came to visit
him, and as they chatted she cheered up and the rain
stopped.   As long as she was happy, the sun would
shine.   Fortunately Mr. Mulally was good at making
her happy.   A cheerful fantasy with bright, appealing
illustrations.

Activities

1) Brainstorm with students this fantasy question.
"What might happen if there were no weather forecasts
--none on the radio or TV, none in the papers, none
at all?"   Would this make any difference in your life?
If so, how?   Would it make any difference in the lives
of others?   Do we really need weather forecasts?

2) Predicting the weather.   Middle- and upper-grade
students will enjoy seeing a copy of the Farmer's
Almanac with its annual weather predictions.   Meteorol-
ogists claim that it is impossible to forecast accurately
the weather on a day-to-day basis one year in advance.
Others claim that the Farmer's Almanac is fairly accurate.   Test the accuracy of the Almanac with that of
your local weather forecast in the paper.   Keep daily
records for one month.   Use a chart similar to this:

WEATHER FORECASTS

Date	Farmer's Almanac	Local Paper	Actual Weather

106 ★ TERBAN, Marvin. Eight Ate: A Feast of Homonym
        Riddles. Illustrated by Giulio Maestro. Houghton
        Mifflin/Clarion, 1982.

Here is another delightful entry into the collection
of books dealing with homonyms and homophones.
Through original riddles the author introduces the concept of confusing words that sound alike but have different meanings. The answer to each riddle is a pair
(or sometimes a trio) of homonyms. The clues are in
the illustrations for visually perceptive youngsters to
find.

Activities

1) Clarify for students the difference between homonyms
(spelled alike, sound alike, different meanings), homophones (sound alike, spelled differently, different meanings), and homographs (spelled alike, pronounced differently, different meanings).
        Examine examples in the book. Are they all homo-
nyms or are homophones also included?

2) Add an example:

HOMONYMS   fair (pretty)   fair (a circus)

_____   _____

_____   _____

_____   _____

HOMOPHONES   sail (as in a boat)   sale (for purchase)

_____   _____

_____   _____

_____   _____

HOMOGRAPHS   conduct (to lead)   conduct (behavior)

_____   _____

_____   _____

_____   _____

107 ★ THALER, Mike. Owly. Illustrated by David Wierner.
        Harper & Row, 1982.

    Owly wants to know everything, and so he asks his
mother to tell him:

        "How many stars are there in the sky?
        How many waves are there in the ocean?
        How high is the sky?"

Wise and lovingly, his mother encourages him to find
the answers for himself and finally asks him a question
of her own. Curious children should see themselves in
Owly and enjoy this gentle, loving story.

Activities

1) Rebus questions: What questions do students want answered? Ask each child to write at least three questions
and to substitute pictures for words when possible.

            How many   are in the

2) Word chains (to promote word fluency): Encourage
students to make word chains using only names of things
found in Owly's forest: OWL
                          E
                          A
                          FOOD
                            E
                            E
                          RABBIT

108 ★ TRAVERS, P. L. Two Pairs of Shoes. Illustrated
        by Leo and Diane Dillon. Viking, 1976.

Here is a tale of contrasts, of two men and their
shoes. One is Abu Kassem, the merchant known for
his riches but also for his ragged slippers, which he
keeps as a visible sign of his miserliness. Ayaz,
once a poor shepherd, now is keeper of the King's
treasures, and also of his old shoes, to remind him
of his once humble station in life. The differing views
of two pairs of shoes reveal much not only about the
two owners but about some basic truths of life.

Activities

1) Discuss: You have just stepped onto an escalator
going up. Where do you arrive? Describe the room,
the land or country. What does it feel like? What
color is it? What does it smell like there?
    What would be a palace to you? What is good about
a palace?
    What means home to you? What feels like home?
Which is better, a palace or a home? Why?
    If you didn't have anything--no bed, radio, toys, or
friends and you could just have one "something," what
would that be?

2) Suggest that the children write a poem by beginning
every other verse with:

    a) I think that I would like _____.

    b) But really I want _____.

3) Let the children draw the land that they would find
at the end of the escalator.

4) Have the children draw or paint the room that they
would most like to live in. ("Your fairy godfriend has
granted you a room all your own. Decorate it in any
way that you would like.")

109 ★ TURKLE, Brinton. Do Not Open. Dutton, 1981.

Miss Moody loved storms, because afterward there
were always wonderful surprises waiting on the beach.
Then she found the mysterious bottle. It was buried

in the sand and said, very distinctly, DO NOT OPEN.
But Miss Moody (who was very curious) did--to more
trouble then she could have imagined!

Activities

1) Here is a modern-day "Pandora's Box." Call attention to the well-known myth and share it with the
class. What similarities and/or differences do the
children see in the two tales?

2) What other tales can children think of that have curiosity as a theme? Children will certainly recall the Curious
George tales, and older students may mention, among
other titles, Louise Fitzhugh's Harriet, the Spy (Harper
& Row, 1964). Plan a class debate on the topic: Curiosity is/is not a desirable trait. The two debating
teams may want to consider:

> Characters whose curiosity has gotten them in
> trouble.

> Characters whose curiosity saved the day.

> What is the difference between curiosity and an
> inquiring mind?

> What discoveries have been made to benefit people
> due to someone's curiosity?

> Does curiosity play an important part in the work
> of an explorer?

110 ★ TURPIN, Lorna. The Sultan's Snakes. Greenwillow,
1979.

The sultan's pet snakes disappeared. He looked all
over for them. His wife, the palace guards, the palace
cleaner--everybody looked and couldn't find them. But
they were there all the time, and clever young readers
will find them on every page! A delightful exercise in
visual perception!

Activities

1) a) What is an interior decorator?

   b) How does a decorator go about planning an
      attractive room?

c) Invite an interior decorator to speak to the class
about his or her work.

d) If you could redecorate your room, or your toy
box, or your closet, what would you do?

2) The Sultan's Snakes is an alliterative title. Alliterative sentences are fun to write and illustrate for all
ages. The longer the sentence is, the more of a tongue
twister it becomes. Children will enjoy trying out each
sentence. A progressive bulletin-board display can be
entitled "Can You Top This" and feature short alliterative sentences appearing first followed by longer and
longer ones. Many students will want to consult dictionaries to vie with each other for the longest sensible
sentence!

111 ★ VAN ALLSBURG, Chris. Jumanji. Houghton Mifflin,
1981.

It seemed like a perfectly normal afternoon when
Judy and Peter's parents went to the opera, leaving
them alone to entertain themselves. To alleviate their
boredom, they set off for a walk in the park, but after
they found the game marked "Jumanji: A Jungle Adventure Game, 'free game, fun for some but not for
all,' " things began to change from the ordinary to the
perfectly extraordinary. By using artistic techniques
different from those he used in his first brilliant book,
The Garden of Abdul Gasazi (Houghton Mifflin, 1979),
Chris Van Allsburg has created magnificent artwork
with an even greater depth, space, and variety of
tone. In both illustrations and text that hauntingly
evoke the surreal, he brings to his readers a vivid
glimpse of the world beyond the Twilight Zone.

Activities

1) Suggest that students choose another part of the
world and develop their own adventure board game.
Question cards about the arctic, the desert, the tropics,
or other areas might allow players who answer correctly to move the number of spaces indicated by dice,
a spinner, or dots on the card. Obstacle cards can
be provided should a player land on an obstacle space
forcing a detour to some well-known place. Obstacles
should be those most frequently encountered in the region.

2) Write the names of as many wild animals as there
are children in your classroom. Write each animal
name on a separate slip and fold or place upside down.
Have each child draw a slip from the pile. Give the
children time to think what it would be like to have the
animals they have drawn for a pet. Give each child
an opportunity to tell the class why or why not the animal would make a good pet. Imaginative answers are
appropriate! After discussing the difficulties of having
a wild animal as a close friend, the children can draw
names of other students in the classroom to be their
"friend for the day."
Classroom discussions on what it would be like to
live where there are no other children might be re-
vealing.

112 ★ WARSHAW, Jerry.   The Funny Drawing Book.   Whit-
        man, 1978.

Young and old alike who think they can't draw will
take heart (and courage) from this "drawing lesson"
with a simple approach. The author uses five basic
shapes: the "artistic circle," (which is a circle drawn
any way you want to draw it), the triangle, the square,
a "bunch of bananas," and the "magic W." He shows
how these basic shapes can be combined to produce
any object.

Activities

1) Shapes can be drawn on the blackboard with students
using their imaginations in combining the shapes into
objects. If blank 16mm film is available, students can
draw directly on the film and produce their own "I
Can't Draw Film." Each object should be drawn twenty-
four times, since 16mm film projects at a rate of
twenty-four frames per second. In drawing on the film,
let students draw any object they wish. Do not strive
for a story line or planned animation on this first attempt.

2) Primary children will enjoy combining the various
shapes in many ways to make pictures. A variation
on drawing shapes might be to give children a large
selection of pre-cut shapes in various sizes and allow
them to experiment with these shapes. Felt cutouts are
ideal for a variety of arrangements on the flannel board.

BY RON WEGEN

balloon trip

113 ★ WEGEN, Ron. Balloon Trip. Houghton Mifflin/
      Clarion, 1981.

    "Get that balloon hot and get it up!" Suddenly two
children and their father are airborne on a daring balloon trip. From their floating basket they first get a
bird's-eye view of city skyscrapers. Then they sweep
across the countryside, over patchworks of farmland.
Without warning, the sky blackens and they find themselves descending to safety, moments ahead of an
Indian summer thunderstorm.

Viewers can share in the excitement the children's
mother feels as she follows the balloon in her red
truck. And, using the illustrator's intricate aerial
perspectives as a guide, they can travel along with
the windriders in this wordless picture book.

Activities

1) Pretend that you are in a balloon flying over the
place where you live. What would you see? How
would things look different if you were viewing them
from high in a balloon? What do you suppose the people in the balloon in this story were thinking about as
they soared high above the ground? What was mother
in the red truck thinking about?

2) Find out about ballooning as a sport. What does a
balloon cost? What does it cost to take a balloon up
for a trip? If there are balloon enthusiasts in your
community, invite one to speak to the class, or, better
yet, take the class to see the balloon! A companion
book that children will enjoy if they want to read more
about balloon flights is Hot-Air Henry, by Mary Calhoun (see entry 19).

114 ★ WEIL, Lisl.   The Story of the Wise Men and the Child.
       Atheneum, 1981.

This is the Christmas story as told in the Gospel
of Matthew. It is the account of the visit of the Wise
Men to Herod the King; their visit to the Child and return to their own land by another way; the flight of
Mary, Joseph, and the Child into Egypt; the killing of
the children of Bethlehem; and the return of the Holy
Family to Nazareth after the death of Herod. The
story is simply and reverently told, and the pictures,
along with the text, make the meaning of the story ac-
cessible to even the youngest children.

Activities

1) Students can do their own illustrated version of this
story to present to others as a holiday program. A
slide show using color-lift slides selected from old
magazines and narrated by several students can provide
a thoughtful holiday program.

2) Students can be led to compare this illustrated story with other illustrated versions of the Christ Child, noting similarities and differences. Perhaps a visit to the class from a person of a different culture or country can be arranged so that children can see the different ways in which Christmas is celebrated.

115 ★ WEISS, Nicki. Waiting. Greenwillow, 1980.

Young children will readily identify with Annalee, who is waiting for her mother to return--for even a few minutes can seem a very long time when you are quite small. But while she waits, Annalee discovers sights and sounds of the out-of-doors, the chirping of a bird, the roses on the fence, the rustling of the grass, a ladybug, the clouds, and the wind blowing. A lovely book to help children savor the beauties of nature with all five senses.

Activities

1) This story might be read twice to the class. The first reading will tell the story and capture the beauty of the language. The second reading will give students a chance to note all of the sights and sounds of the meadow. Let each student choose one living thing (plant or animal) found around a meadow and find out more about it. Illustrations and information can be pasted on the bulletin board or compiled into a class book on meadow life.

2) To promote attentive listening, ask the children to count the number of things Annalee discovers in the story. How many names can they remember? Ask the librarian to gather a collection of easy nonfiction on pond or forest creatures for the classroom reading table. If available, obtain Encyclopaedia Britannica's World of Animals tape/book series and allow children to spend time listening to the tapes and following the texts in the books.

116 ★ WEISSMAN, Sam Q. An Apple to Eat or Cross the Street. Prentice-Hall, 1980.

When is a hat not a hat? When it is a mountain

full of cowboys hiding from Indians? Imaginative and
practical uses of common objects dear to childhood--
from a brush to a banana to a hat--are inventively described and illustrated on facing pages in this original
and charming introduction to situations and circum-
stances where the eye and the mind meet.

Activities

1) Brainstorm: How many uses can you think of for
a pencil, a pin, a brick, a frying pan, a bed sheet,
a comb, a cup?
    What unusual use did each child think of that no one
else thought of?

2) Draw a picture or write a story about an object you
would invent if you had nothing else to do on a rainy
afternoon.
    Assume that your invention has been granted a patent
by the U.S. Patent Office. List the materials you need
to put your invention into production. Make a flow
chart or write the directions for assembling your invention.

117 ★ WESTON, Martha. Peony's Rainbow. Lothrop, Lee &
          Shepard, 1981.

    Peony Pig had always wanted a rainbow of her own,
so one day she just took one! Then the trouble began.
The rainbow escapes and Peony discovers how many
places a rainbow can be found--in balloons, hats, skirts,
a lasso, and finally in a lake of tears. Here is a
story for looking at and for reading, again and again.

Activities

1) Discuss: Do some people make you feel like a
prism? How? Do they let different colors or parts
of you shine out?
    How can we help to make everyone we meet be
rainbows?
    What color are you?
    If you were a rainbow, where would you hide?

2) Bring some prisms into the classroom. Let the
children make rainbows. Talk about what it is that

the prism does in changing the white light into colors.
Have the children make rainbow mobiles. Taking colored pieces of wool, all of differing lengths, hang different shapes of rainbows.

Keep your eye out for possible rainbow weather so
that the class will be able to see one.

Hide the six rainbow colors all around the room.
Have the children try to pick out as many as they can.

3) Using oil-based clay, let the children make a design (clothes pegs are handy for this) in their own ball
of clay. Have them dip this into rainbow colors of
paint, then print into paper to make designs.

4) Let the children make flowers for each color of the
rainbow. Use these to string around the room or to
decorate the edges of bulletin boards.

118 ★ WILDE, Oscar. The Star Child. Illustrated by Fiona
French. Four Winds, 1979.

Two woodcutters were making their way home one
snowy evening when a bright star fell out of the sky
and into the pine forest before them. They ran toward
it, and found not a star but a sleeping baby wrapped
in a cloak of golden tissue. One of the men took the
baby home. The child was brought up with the village
children, and every year he grew more beautiful, but
he also became vain and selfish. As the child of a
star, he was filled with overweening pride. One day
he accidentally met his real mother, but when she
called him her son he spurned her because she was
old and ugly and clothed in rags. For this cruel act
he was transformed into a creature as ugly as a toad.
What happened when the Star Child wanders through
his medieval world learning humility and compassion
makes a moving story highlighted by jewel-like illustrations.

Activities

1) Discuss: Have you ever done anything that was quite
unlike you? What did you do?

What is it that makes friends like us?

Why don't we have to worry how we look around
friends?

What was the Star Child's gift? Why is it special
when we offer ourselves or make gifts instead of buy-
ing them?

2) Hold a sharing party. Everyone in the class is in-
vited, including you, to bring something that is special
to them to share. It might be a story, poem, a picture, a song, a dance. This is not so much a "show
and tell" as a chance for the children to appreciate
each other's uniqueness.

3) Have the children make a bookmark for a friend.
Collect and dry leaves and paste these onto a strip of
colored construction paper.

119 ★ WILLIAMS, Jay. The Reward Worth Having. Illus-
        trated by Mercer Mayer. Four Winds, 1976.

Three soldiers marching home discover a tiny little
man in trouble and set him free. For their kindness
the man allows each to choose his own reward from a
treasure chamber. The first soldier chooses an iron
bird because of its strength. The second chooses a
golden bird because of its value. The third chooses a
small gray bird, very much alive. What reward was
most truly worth having? As the king's soldiers discover, it depends on what you value most in life.

Activities

1) Discuss: What is a foolish person?
    Have you ever made a mistake or a wrong decision?
Were you ever foolish? What can you do to prevent
making the same mistakes a second time?
    What is meant by the saying "The best things in
life are free"?
    What is meant by the saying "All that glitters is
not gold"?
    Do you think spoiling someone is the best way to
take care of him or her?
    Do you think people always get what they deserve?

2) Interview people and find out what they value most
in life. Then rank the results in order from most
valued to least valued. Discuss this information in
relation to such issues as city, national, and world

problems. Devise plans or schemes in which the
problems can be lessened. For example, one most-
valued need people have is the need for good health.
Problems that exist may be high medical costs and
diseases without cures. What would be your plan to
help solve the problem?

3) Become acquainted with things that people place
much value on, such as paintings, sculpture, literary
works, or music, and find out how they compare with
other types of art that do not receive wide acclaim.
Share your research in informal discussion groups.
Also arrange for trips to museums, galleries, etc.,
for firsthand experience.

120 ★ WILLIAMS, Jay. The Surprising Things Maui Did. Illus-
      trated by Charles Mikolaycak. Four Winds, 1979.

This ancient legend is told with spare text and powerful full-color illustrations. It is the tale of Maui, who
returns to the islands after living with the Sea God to
create a land in which his people could live. He played
his drum and the birds appeared in the trees. He
lifted the sky so that it lay high in the heavens. He
captured the sun in a net and made it go more slowly
so that the land would be warm. This Hawaiian tale
of creation is an interesting contrast to other tales,
and with older children it might be followed by a reading aloud of Armstrong Sperry's Call It Courage
(Macmillan, 1940).

Activities

1) For older students this book can provide a beautiful
introduction to a unit of nature study, ecology, the origin of the earth, or oceanography. As the book is
read, students should be aware of the way in which the
author poetically interprets the physical world. Students can be urged to learn about how islands are
formed or about the kinds of life found on arctic and
on tropical islands. A table display contrasting the
plant and animal life on islands in various parts of the
world should lead students to a greater understanding
of the relationship of climate and plant and animal life.

2) As the story is read to them, younger students can
be asked to name only those things that are found in

the ocean or only things that are found on an island.
An activity sheet can be prepared in advance entitled
the "ABC's of the Ocean." After hearing the story,
students can fill in letters with names of plants or
animals that were mentioned in the story, then visit
the school library to look at other books on ocean life
to complete as many other letters as they can.

121 ★ WILLIAMS, Kit. Masquerade. Schocken, 1980.

Author-artist Williams has created an intriguing
mystery for readers of all ages, as they ponder difficult riddles that can eventually lead the successful to
a real treasure buried somewhere in Britain. Here
is a richly illustrated tale of a rabbit supposedly carrying a jewel from the moon through earth, air, fire,
and water to the sun. A solution to all the riddles
leads the reader to a jewel-encrusted golden hare.
Williams has claimed that a ten-year-old can solve the
mystery--but in the end it was an adult who actually
found the treasure!

Activities

1) Though this complex fantasy is not intended for very
young children, most will enjoy the literal interpretation of the tale and be ready for a riddle game of their
own. Riddles on the bulletin board can serve as clues
to useful items hidden around the classroom (pencils,
erasers, handkerchiefs). The child who thinks he or
she can answer a riddle is allowed to try before the
search begins. In this game finders are keepers!

2) Many picture-book artists have included treasures
to be found in their illustrations. In Anno's Journey
(Collins and World, 1978), by Mitsumasa Anno, treasures
abound! Make the book available for browsing. Challenge students to add their discoveries to a classroom
chart. This can be a year-long project.

TREASURES IN ANNO'S JOURNEY

Famous Paintings	Famous People	Famous Tales
La Grande Jatte	Beethoven	Sleeping Beauty
The Gleaners	John Wayne	Emperor's New Clothes
The Angelus		Don Quixote

122 ★ WILLIAMS, Margery. The Velveteen Rabbit. Double-
       day, 1958.

A classic and sensitive story on how toys become
real. A beloved stuffed rabbit is a little boy's con-
stant companion. The rabbit learns from another toy,
the skin-horse, about becoming real. "Real isn't how
you are made. It's a thing that happens to you. When
a child loves you a long, long time, not just to play
with but REALLY loves you, then you become real."
The rabbit sadly learns that one doesn't become real
until "most of your hair has been loved off, and your
eyes drop out and you get loose in the joints and very
shabby." After the little boy has a bout with scarlet
fever, all of his toys and picture books are taken outside to be burned. The battered velveteen rabbit sheds
a tear over his fate, but the magic that results from
his real tear turns him into a real rabbit for ever and
ever.

Activities

1) Ask the children if they ever had an especially loved
toy that became real. Find out if they still have such
a beloved toy at home, tucked away in a closet, which
they could bring to school. These old friends could
sit along the edge of the chalkboard or table. Children
who no longer have such toys can draw pictures of
them and post them beside the others. Give each child
an opportunity to tell how his or her toy became real,
when it happened, and how it happened. Some children
might rather write the story, which could then be posted
beside the toy or picture. Help the children to see the
fun of reminiscing, and of using their imaginations. To
help the class get started, the teacher might be the
first to share memories of a beloved plaything.

2) For older classes a great creative writing project
can be initiated on the topic of "What became of my
Teddy Bear?" (or bride doll, or bulldozer, or whisk-
ered mouse). Encourage the children to let their imaginations run freely for delightful and un-self-conscious
stories.

123 ★ WINTERINGHAM, Victoria. Penguin Day. Harper &
       Row, 1982.

Here is a visual delight for young viewers as they
follow the antics of a group of madcap penguins.

"No birdwatcher has ever seen them.
No explorer has ever discovered them.
Nobody in the world has spent a day with them. "

But young children will discover a busy world filled
with action and humor as the penguins get up in the
morning, bathe, have a most unconventional breakfast,
and embark on a day that includes school, skating,
singing, parties, and a host of other activities. These
are not pages to flip through quickly, but to pour over
in discovering the many visual delights to be found.

Activity

The author/illustrator had many problems to solve
in depicting the daily lives of an imaginary group of
penguins. How many questions can students answer
before discovering the author's solutions to these problems?

a) What should penguins wear?

b) What kind of exercises should penguins do?

c) How will a mother penguin feed her young?

d) What will penguins need to learn at school?

e) What kind of games will penguins play?

f) How do older penguins entertain their younger
brothers and sisters?

g) What would be a good penguin song?

h) Why would penguins give a party? What party
games will they play?

Encourage divergent, imaginative responses.

124 ★ WOLKSTEIN, Diane. The Banza: A Haitian Story.
Illustrated by Marc Brown. Dial, 1981.

When Teegra, a little tiger, and Cabree, a little

goat, find shelter together during a fierce storm, they
become fast friends.   As they part, Teegra gives
Cabree a banza, a little banjo, and tells her, "It will
protect you.   The banza belongs to the heart, and there
is no stronger protection than the heart." Cabree does
not understand, and she goes trotting on her way, stop-
ping now and then to play a tune on her banza.   Before
long, though, she finds herself in grave danger and discovers that her banza does indeed have special powers.

Activities

1) Haiti is an island.   Island life can be very different
from life on the mainland.   Suppose you lived on an
island: How would your life be different?   Consider:
Food, Clothing, Recreation, Travel, Work of the people.

2) Select one island country.   Make an ABC book telling about the place you choose.   Divide each page in
your book into four quarters.   Place the letters of the
alphabet in the upper-left-hand corner of each quarter.
Name and illustrate one word beginning with each letter
that tells about your island country.   Share your books
with other classes.

125 ★ ZOLOTOW, Charlotte.   The Song.   Illustrated by Nancy
        Tafuri.   Greenwillow, 1982.

   A well-known picture-book author presents a delightfully descriptive, child's-eye view of the four seasons.
"One day Susan woke up with the song of a little bird
inside her.   'Listen,' she said to her mother and father.
But neither of them heard.   And they didn't hear the
song when it changed from a summer song to a fall
song, and then to a winter song.   But Susan went on
listening.   And in the spring, walking home from school,
she met a friend.   'Listen,' she said, and the two of
them listened."   The large, bright illustrations are especially suited to viewing by young children and clarify
the text, which is not oversimplified for young listeners.

Activity

   Season Collage: Using old magazines, children can
look for and cut out signs of the four seasons.   Several mentioned in the text are:

flowers	butterflies	rain
green meadows	birds	maple leaves
pumpkins	goldenrod	cold winds
snowflakes	frosty windows	wood fires
pine trees	mistletoe	holly
toasted marshmallows	violets	silky new grass
apple blossoms		

Separate the pictures into four groups, one for each
season. Fold paper in half and in half again to make
four squares. Paste parts of the pictures in each
square to create a four-seasons collage.

126 ★ ZOLOTOW, Charlotte. The White Marble. Illustrated
by Deborah Ray. Harper & Row, 1982.

On a summer night in a city park two children find
a special friendship that transforms the world around
them into a private enchantment. They feel the soft
grass, the fountain spraying cool water on their faces,
the breeze from an approaching rainstorm rustling
golden leaves--and it is all theirs. From the moment
John Henry finds a shiny white marble until the final
good-byes of the children and their parents, the reader
sees the natural world through the eyes of children and
romps with them through the park in the dusk.

Activity

Here is a book filled with vivid description. Children hear the "soft echo of footsteps"; smell the "air,
fresh and sweet"; feel the "little rain wind ruffling their
hair"; and see "the water fountain sprinkling up white
and foamy in the night." Orally, or through written
descriptions, change the scene as it might become when
the approaching storm hits. What would the children
hear, feel, see, and smell in relation to:

a) the bench
b) the lamplight
c) tree branches
d) the grass
e) the sky

f) lilac bushes
g) the water fountain
h) the lamplit path
i) leaves

Part II
CHILDREN INTERPRET LITERATURE THROUGH ART AND MEDIA

INTEGRATING ART AND LITERATURE EXPERIENCES

Despite modern technology and the increasing use of audio-visual media in education, the storyhour continues to be an important part of every school day in many classrooms. Teachers and librarians have long known the value of sharing a treasured book with boys and girls and of developing that feeling of oneness with a class that comes from laughing or crying together over the fate of a particular hero or heroine.

Because children's books cover an infinite variety of ideas and topics, they belong in every area of the curriculum, yet many teachers have overlooked this most valuable of resources by relegating fine children's books to a specific daily or weekly story time. Among the many activities that can emerge from the sharing of a book are imaginative games, research projects, creative writing, pantomime, puppetry, live drama, musical composition, children's poetry, field trips, nature walks, and a wide variety of art projects.

The integration of art and literature experiences follows so naturally that it is surprising that such activities have not become a part of every school art program. A fine picture book is, in itself, a perfect blend of art and literature where literary and artistic talents combine to make a perfect whole. Marjorie Hamlin's statement in the introduction bears repeating here:

> We cannot overlook the fact that many picture books are valuable as artworks alone. Surely, children's books are blessed immeasurably today by the number of outstanding artists who are using their talents and time for the young. The variety of media that are used in producing books of dramatic color and exquisite quality is astonishing. Many picture books can be shared simply as a series of artworks that can lift and mold children's tastes for the very best. Be sure that your students have time to browse and

absorb the form and line and color that these artists have provided for them. It is possible that
one evocative page of beauty may stay with a child
forever, as a yardstick upon which he or she unconsciously measures what is worthy against what
is trivial.

The basic purposes of literature and art are entirely
compatible. Both literature and art help to build within the
child fortunate enough to be exposed to the two media a growing sense of awareness. Literature experiences and art experiences help children to become aware of the world that
surrounds them, to find beauty in the simplest of life's plea-
sures and to develop compassion and understanding for their
fellow human beings. Great writers and great artists who
have achieved any measure of acceptance and fame have done
so because they were able to transmit their awareness of life
to others.

The integration of literature and art allows students to
go beyond the books and creatively to change, rearrange, or

add to the elements of a story to produce imaginative works that reveal their own sense of awareness and allow them to interpret this to others.

Teachers or librarians who do not themselves feel competent to direct art activities in the classroom often omit these valuable experiences from the children's activities. Yet it is in the classroom that art experiences can truly happen. "Art" cannot be turned on and become a part of a child's total awareness during a forty-five-minute art class with an overworked art teacher pushing around a paint cart for a monthly "painting" session.

The pages that follow are for those teachers and librarians who are willing to discover for themselves the unique value that can be found in the integration of literature and art. Step-by-step directions are included for incorporating a wide variety of art experiences in the literature program. The techniques are applicable not only to the books described in E IS FOR EVERYBODY but to any treasured favorite that is shared with children.

1

DRAWING AND PAINTING

DRAWING WITH CRAYONS

Crayon drawings are just right for that magic moment when young illustrators have been inspired by Jerry Warshaw's The Funny Drawing Book (entry 112) to try their hand at using basic shapes to compose a picture; or are anxious to create unusual shopkeepers after sharing Anita and Arnold Lobel's On Market Street (entry 65); or perhaps are ready to illustrate their own poetry after laughing together over Lenore Blegvad's The Parrot in the Garret and Other Rhymes About Dwellings (entry 16). Many moments such as these occur when literature is shared, and the ready availability and ease of use of crayons as an art medium can help to keep these moments alive.

Suggest that students try these variations:

1) Use a peeled broken crayon and color in PART of your shapes with the SIDE of the crayon. Do another part of the shapes with the POINT of the crayon, pressing very hard, especially for smaller shapes.

2) Do the basic drawing with only ONE crayon. When it is completed, take another color and go over the same lines again, putting the second color right BESIDE the first color.

3) Choose one part of your drawing that can be broken into shapes. For example: if your drawing is of an animal, the head is one shape, the body another, the legs still another. Color each shape a different color and use the side of your crayon on part of it.

4) Color your entire picture. That's right, THE WHOLE THING! Use the side of your crayon for part of it.

126

5) When your crayon drawing is completed, take it to the watercolor table and paint over it with one color of watercolor.

6) If your drawing is of an animal, put bars all the way from the top of your page to the bottom. (Make the bars nice and straight so the animal can't slip through.) OR put buildings behind a tall fence or draw five tall trees with a few bare branches from the bottom of the paper to the top.

DRAWING WITH FELT-TIP MARKERS

Provision should be made in the classroom for impromptu art projects for individual students who have experienced that magic moment that comes from great literature. A special bulletin-board area should be set aside for this purpose and materials kept in a handy place for use by budding artists. Best materials for use in this "spur of the moment" type of activity are precut paper squares kept in a box in a convenient area and felt-tip markers. A student who has a picture in mind from some exciting story, or a "dream" to tell, or perhaps simply has a spare minute to "fool around" should get a paper square and a marker or two to work with. Have available also precut construction paper for mounting. If the marker drawings are all to be the result of a literature activity, use an appropriate heading for the bulletin board. For example, student pictures from well-known fairy tales can be captioned "ALL IN A KNIGHT'S WORK"!

Crayon Techniques

Color hard with the point.

"Rub" an area with the
side of the crayon.

Do a drawing with one
color of crayon, go
"around" same lines
with another color of
crayon.

Break up all spaces and fill
with different colors.

Draw "bars" over the
entire drawing. A fence
over city buildings or
"trees" over a landscape.

Put a watercolor "wash"
over a crayon drawing
(only one color).

EASEL, TABLE, AND DESK PAINTING

Getting Started. The moment is ripe for initiating a
painting project when children have
shared such books as Charlotte Zolotow's The Song (entry 125),
a delightfully descriptive child's-eye view of the four seasons,
or have used the unusual shoe in Rodney Peppe's The Mice
Who Lived in a Shoe (entry 84) as a starting point for design-
ing their own unique houses. The bright yellows and blues in
Robert Kalen's Jump, Frog, Jump (entry 55) should inspire
young painters to create their own versions of pond life. Almost any fine picture book can serve as a starting point in
stimulating the artist that exists in the heart and mind of
every child.

Whether using one of these books or any other favorite,
it is important to initiate a class discussion while children are
excited and have pictures in their minds. Discuss their mind
pictures with such questions as "What pictures come to your
mind from this book? Were all the dragons the same shape?
Is there one best shape for a dragon? Do dragons come in
a variety of colors? What colors do you remember? Are
there any other things you see when you think about the story?"

As children mention various objects, talk about shapes.
If you are uncertain as to the shape of an object, ask a student to volunteer to draw it on the blackboard for further clarifi-
cation. Let children help each other by their descriptions,
board drawings, and discussions. As the discussion continues,
cover desks and pass out brushes, old magazines for palettes,
sponges, and paper. The directions that follow are provided
to ensure success in the initial and subsequent painting activities.

Easel Painting. The value of painting cannot be overem-
phasized, provided it is handled in a
free and easy manner with students. Preparation to minimize
mess and accidents is essential to a good painting program.
Such preparation lessens confusion and promotes a creative
atmosphere.

The painting space must be arranged in such a manner
that students can move about without entering each other's
spaces. Tables, desks, or easels must be arranged so that
students can leave the painting area without bumping others.
If possible, students should have both kinds of painting experiences, table and easel.

If an easel area is available, cover the floor with an old cloth rug used only for that purpose. It can be rolled when not in use.

Easel painting can be handled as an on-going daily activity. Set up a procedure so that each student has time at the easel sometime during the week. Motivate students by praise and by displaying paintings in attractive ways. Praise the correct use of materials, the subject matter of a painting,

and neatness, as well as the finished work.   Minimize a
ruined picture with "I'm sure all artists feel that way sometimes."   If disaster occurs every time a particular student
paints, look for the cause.   Watch the student's efforts closely
and give a feeling of success by saying, "Oh Robby, stop now!
That is really good!"   Take the picture off the easel, praise
it before the other students and hang it for all to see.   Nothing succeeds like success!

     Illustrated below is a simple easel that can be con-
veniently constructed and stored.   Needed for its construction
are four pieces of wood 1"x2" and 45" long, two 2" hinges

with screws, four screw eyes, two pieces of heavy string about a yard long, and two large pieces of cardboard.

Hinge each pair of 1-by-2s together at one end. Put screw eyes in the sides of each pair about one foot from the opposite end of the hinges. These are the easel legs. To set up the easel, staple the cardboard to the easel on both sides. Tie the string between the screw eyes of each leg to prevent its unfolding.

Staple the paper to the cardboard for each painter. The cardboard can be easily changed or removed for storage.

Use juice cans for paint containers. Use only a small amount of paint at a time--add more as needed. Use a different brush for each color and clean brushes at the end of the painting session. This is essential for the life of the brushes.

Table or Desk Painting. Table or desk painting is a different process. It is particularly good when all children are painting at the same time. Materials needed:

1) a paint shirt (a parent's old one with sleeves cut off);

2) newspaper to cover the table or desks;

3) two paper towels or a sponge;

4) containers for water (butter tubs or empty pint milk cartons);

5) paper to paint on (be sure the student's name is on the back before he or she begins);

6) a disposable palette made out of a page from a slick-paper magazine (see illustration);

7) tempera paint already mixed (plastic soap dispensers can be used as squeeze bottles);

8) bristle brushes with long handles and $\frac{1}{2}$"-wide bristles;

9) teaspoons to dispense paint if jar tempera is used;

10) a bucket of water resting on some newspapers to deposit used paint brushes.

Palettes are made from
slick magazine paper.

Dispense paint directly from
the jars of liquid tempera

or squeeze out a blob
from a detergent bottle
directly onto the palette.

If detergent squeeze bottles are used, leave a tiny bit
of detergent in the bottle, since a little soap in the paint makes
for easy cleaning of brushes at the end of the session.   Responsible students can assist in dispensing paint.   Individual
student palettes can be made by folding $\frac{1}{2}$" of the edge of several magazine pages to prevent paint from running off onto the
desks.   Explain to students that a palette is used by artists
to mix their colors.

Water for cleaning brushes can be eliminated if each
student places a piece of newspaper under the palette.   Excess
paint can be brushed onto the paper when a color change is
desired.   Urge students not to "fill" their brushes unless they

are sure that much paint is needed.   It is easier to get more
paint than to get rid of the excess.   When everyone has made
a palette, give each student a teaspoon of the colors to be
used or a squirt from the dispenser bottle.   As paint is dis-
pensed, talk about an artist's palette, how the painter uses
it to mix paints and yet keep the original colors.   A sample
explanation follows:

> "Take a small amount of paint from one side of a
> color.   Put it in a bare spot on your palette.   Take
> a small amount from another color and put on the
> same bare spot.   Mix the paints.   Notice that you
> still have your original colors. "

Urge students to keep their original colors clean by taking
paint from the side of their color blobs for mixing.   These
directions may need to be repeated often during the first few
sessions until students learn control.

Encourage young artists to fill the entire page with
paint, to tuck in one color beside another and not to forget
the background.   After paintings are dry, instruct students
to "go around" shapes that "get lost" with a felt-tip marker
or crayon.

Mixing Colors.   Using different combinations of paints
with students can be a stimulating
color-discovery method.   If paints always are red, yellow,
and blue, students have ALL of the colors, which can be confusing.   Try some of the following combinations.   Use only
the colors given and discuss the result of the mixtures.   This
is particularly good when table-painting with magazine pages
as palettes.   Mixing is much more exciting.   Try:

Turquoise, white, and yellow   Blue, orange, and white
Red, green, and white   Orange, black, and yellow
Turquoise, orange, and white   Black and white
Turquoise, yellow, orange,   Magenta, violet, and yellow
   and white   Red, yellow, brown, and
Violet, yellow, and white   white
Violet, yellow, and blue   Red, yellow, and white

Don't tell students what colors will result.   Let them discover!
Then discuss their results.

Other Materials for Painting.   Changes in materials
used in painting can be

very stimulating and motivating in themselves. Try some of
these ideas:

1) Use colored construction paper with tempera paint: gray
   or light blue for winter scenes, orange or peach for fall
   scenes, and let some of the paper show through for sky
   or ground.

2) Use tempera paint on newspaper. Classified sections
   are best. Try this for Halloween, that all-important,
   favorite time for elementary students.

3) Use "sugar chalk" instead of paint on manila or colored
   construction paper. Soak colored chalk in small containers of water with two tablespoons of sugar for about
   one hour. Pour off the excess water and cover tightly
   until ready for use. Chalk will keep for about one week
   before it starts getting moldy. The chalk flows like a
   stick of paint and adheres well to the paper.

4) Monoprints can be made with fingerpaint placed directly
   on a desk- or tabletop. The entire hand is used to
   spread the paint to paper size. Push the paint hard
   with different parts of the hand, allowing the desk to
   show through. Lay a sheet of paper over the painting
   and press. The painting is transferred to the paper.
   Clean up with sponges.

   Cleaning Up. When painting with a whole classroom,
   cleanup can be accomplished in an or-
derly and nonchaotic way. Here are some suggestions teachers
have found helpful.

   Appoint a person or two to collect water in large cans;
brushes can be collected at the same time. Paintings should
be carefully carried to a drying spot previously designated.
Fold the used palette into the cover paper and appoint a trash-
pickup person. Have six or seven damp rags or damp sponges
to pass to each person for finger cleanup. This prevents students from mobbing the sink and washing and washing and
washing. Appoint someone to make sure the sink area is
clean, and you check the brushes after the brush monitor has
done his or her task. To care for brushes properly, have a
bucket or a No. 3-size coffee can containing warm soapy water
to deposit soiled brushes. Shortly after the end of the painting
session slosh the brushes up and down vigorously in the warm
soapy water, then follow with a thorough rinsing. Stand the
brushes on their handles to dry.

MOUNTING STUDENT WORK

Mounting student work is important. Everything looks better when it has been attractively framed or mounted. The following ideas may prove helpful in accomplishing this time- and material-consuming task.

1) Cut a sheet of construction paper from the opposite corners and mount the picture with these corners extended as shown. This is very attractive and takes less paper than other methods.

2) Carefully trim the edges from a picture and mount it on colored construction paper of the same size, making a frame. Use rubber cement or staple the picture at the corners.

3) Check with young artists on some part of their work that might be trimmed to make small pictures. "John,

this cat is really good in this painting.   Let's trim off
the rest and mount it, OK?"   Be sure to ask.   A student may not want a painting trimmed, in which case,
DON'T !

Construction paper cut from corner to corner; mount behind
picture.   Or mount trimmed picture on larger sheets of construction paper: two sheets in contrasting colors are very
attractive.

2.

DISPLAYS

COLLAGES AND MOSAICS

The unique quality of some children's books demands
an unusual style of illustration. The very nature of a collage
or mosaic requires a subject that is highly imaginative and
not easily defined. Two books that are especially appropriate
to share with students as springboards to activities in collage
are Isadora's Ben's Trumpet (entry 54) and the Lobels' On
Market Street (entry 66).

In Ben's Trumpet artist Rachel Isadora unifies diverse
images found in music through the use of shapes and shadows.
After the small boy Ben listens to the jazz musicians, the
rhythm stays with him all the way home. A feeling for tone
and rhythm can come through a collage interpretation of a
particular piece of music or of the sounds of a specific instrument.

The Lobels' On Market Street is a delightful exercise
in fluency as the artist combined diverse wares to create a
composite picture of the merchant who sells them. Children
will enjoy making computer-age collages by creating the seller
of computers out of computer parts; or by depicting the video-
game salesman out of the variety of video games available.

From the world of nature imagine quiet collages inspired by Kevin Henkes's All Alone (entry 46), with such
images as a flower bending in the wind, a bug crawling on a
window, or other quiet images that come from careful obser-
vation.

Imagine, too, a classroom display of mosaic dragons
that could result from a sharing of Seidelman and Mintonye's
The Fourteenth Dragon (Harlin Quist, 1968; see first edition
of E IS FOR EVERYBODY, page 65). Colors, textures, and

materials for each dragon will vary greatly as the students, inspired by seeing the interpretation of thirteen different artists' dragons in the book, exercise their imaginations to the fullest.

Using the simple techniques that follow, both teachers and students should find the creation of collages and mosaics a rewarding activity.

Ideas for Making Collages.   Materials needed:

1) base or frame of cardboard; a shoe-box lid will work well;

2) adhesives--glue for metal or wood, paste for cloth or paper, stapler for heavier materials, cloth or leather;

3) combinations of materials--things that are pleasing to touch with variety in size, shape, texture, and color. Consider materials that are rough, smooth, bright, dull, patterned, and plain; large and small objects; and things that make lines, such as string, yarn, and ribbon, which can be moved in and out and around to make pathways for the design.

Materials should be sorted into categories.   Best work will result if color is used as a unifying device.   Each student should decide on a basic color and try to stick to that color with its shades and tones.   The student selects appropriate materials from the various categories and begins to arrange and change the shapes within the collage.   Materials should not be glued or fastened until several arrangements have been tried.   In experimenting with different arrangements, the student should:

Repeat some materials	Repeat some shapes
Repeat some exact colors	Use some lines
Vary the shades of colors	Vary some textures

When the student is satisfied with the arrangement, materials are fastened to the cardboard background with the appropriate adhesive.   The cardboard should be trimmed and mounted on a larger background with the appropriate adhesive. The cardboard should be trimmed and mounted on a larger background or frame of appropriate material.

Magazine Collage.   Themes for a magazine collage
                     can evolve from either realistic
or imaginative works of fiction.   Various kinds of magazines
pertaining to the subject chosen should be available.   Pictures
are cut or torn into a variety of shapes.   Use construction
paper for mounting.   A unity of theme can be achieved with
cut construction paper letters or letters cut from the theme
pictures themselves.   Do not forget lines either between the
shapes or around the letters.   The lines should lead in and
around the shapes to unify the collage.   For permanency,
coat with polymer and mount on a plain colored background.

Paper Mosaics.   Materials needed for torn- or cut-
                  paper mosaics are:

1) scrap construction paper, wrapping paper, or wallpaper;

2) construction paper of various sizes for the background
   (Allow children to select the size on which they want to
   develop their mosaic.);

3) glue, paste, or rubber cement;

4) scissors.

In preparation for this activity sort papers by color
and cut them into manageable shapes.   Store by color in butter tubs or shoe boxes.

Using a dark color of construction paper for the background, the student should draw the shape of a single animal

Draw shape on dark
construction paper;

fill in the shape (and the
background) with bits of
colored paper, leaving
spaces between the bits.

or figure.   This can be done with chalk, crayon, or felt-tip
marker.   The basic shape should be kept as simple as possible.   The student spreads a small amount of glue at a time
within the shape and begins to fit upon it small pieces of
colored paper.   The mosaic is more successful if a small
amount of background is allowed to show between each piece.
The finished mosaic should be coated with polymer and mounted
on a contrasting background.   Allow considerable time for a
mosaic project--usually several forty-five-minute periods are
required.

BULLETIN BOARDS

Bulletin boards can be used to introduce a particular
type of literature (animal stories, myths, etc.) in order to
stimulate curiosity about an author or type of story.   They
can also spark student interest and questions and serve as a
means through which students can interpret a favorite work

of literature to others. The construction of an attractive and
meaningful board requires, in addition to a creative approach,
the use of many basic research techniques. The subject of
the board must be defined and clarified. Material in keeping
with the basic idea or concept of the board must be gathered
or created, and organized so that the overall concept or idea
is easily grasped by the viewer. Not only must the central
theme be easily seen but it must be presented with unity,
balance, and purpose. Artistically the board should be of
good composition, eye-catching, colorful, in good taste, and
uncluttered.

Fine children's books that can serve as springboards
to total class involvement in the construction of delightful bulletin boards are:

Aruego, José, and Dewey, Ariane. We Hide, You Seek
(entry 7). From this delightful introduction to camouflage
students can create an authentic setting (pond, meadow,
desert) in which their paper animals can hide.

Balian, Lorna. Leprechauns Never Lie (entry 9). After
helping the leprechaun in this story save his pot of gold,
students can use the pattern provided to make their own
pots of gold filled with wishes for a "What's Your Wish"
bulletin board.

Calhoun, Mary. Hot-Air Henry (entry 19). Create your own
tall-tale character or exaggerated situation for a thought-
provoking, fun bulletin-board display!

Cohen, Miriam. Jim Meets the Thing (entry 26). The children's own rare creatures can be created from pictures of
common objects through elaboration. Names and couplets
about the creatures can complete the bulletin-board display.

Craig, M. Jean. The Man Whose Name Was Not Thomas
(entry 27). Imagine a bulletin board entitled "KEEP HAPPY"
that would show the children's posters of their favorite activities.

dePaola, Tomie. The Hunter and the Animals (entry 30).
Create a construction-paper tree for the bulletin board.
Have the tree come back to life by allowing children to
add a green leaf every time one of them gives of him- or
herself to help another.

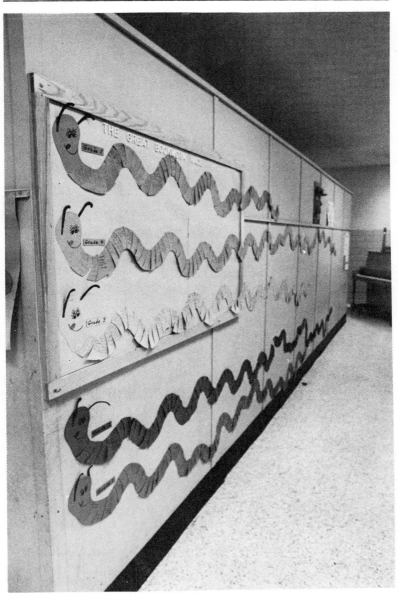

The Great Bookworm Race (five grades; books read)

dePaola, Tomie. Strega Nona (entry 31). A Halloween bulletin board of good witches, along with a good spell she
might have, is a new twist for celebrating this holiday.

Florian, Douglas. The City (entry 37). This busy book can
stimulate picture words having to do with the city. A
bulletin-board city of picture words will enhance a unit of
study on community helpers.

Goodall, John S. Paddy's New Hat (entry 42). Create a
wordless cartoon story as long as your bulletin board!
Students can work in teams in adding drawings and dialogue
to the longest comic strip in the school!

Turpin, Lorna. The Sultan's Snakes (entry 110). A progressive bulletin board display can be entitled "CAN YOU TOP
THIS?" with short alliterative sentences appearing first,
topped by longer and longer tongue twisters.

        Constructing a Bulletin Board. In constructing a bulle-
                                        tin board, a variety of
approaches can be taken.   If, for example, the class under-
takes a jungle bulletin board from We Hide, You Seek, the
board might first be covered with a large sheet of colored
paper. (Colored paper comes on large rolls and is a good
investment for any school or library.) A committee of students can do the background.   Each class member can draw
or cut out a camouflage animal and place the animal in its
hiding place on the board.   Background colors should be noted
so that animals can be painted or colored appropriately to
blend with the setting.

TABLETOPS AND DIORAMAS

        Table displays and dioramas can result from the shar-
ing of almost any children's book.   Hans Christian Andersen's
The Snow Queen (entry 4) describes the icy North, where the
Queen rules with an equally icy heart.   A description of a
winter table scene is presented as Activity 3 in that entry.

        Other displays of objects from nature can result from
nature walks or field trips following a reading of books designed to develop awareness and appreciation of nature.   Among
the best of the newer titles are: The Hunter and the Animals,

by Tomie dePaola (entry 30); Something Wonderful Happened, by Janet Givens (entry 41); All Alone, by Kevin Henkes (entry 46); The Star Rocker, by Joseph Slate (entry 104); Waiting, by Nicki Weiss (entry 115); and The White Marble, by Charlotte Zolotow (entry 126).

The possibilities for both displays and dioramas are endless, as children depict scenes from favorite books or build upon the knowledge gained from a book that has been shared.

Tabletops. Table displays can be an attractive addition to any classroom. One area should be set aside for use as a display corner. In this area should be placed a small table, a piece of neutral-color material, a few empty cardboard boxes, masking tape to hold things in place, and straight pins.

To set up the display area, tape the boxes to the table, placing larger boxes in the back. Graduate the sizes so that there are steps in the arrangement. Drape the material over the entire box arrangement and pin it to the boxes. Add color with construction paper on the cloth and urge students to bring in their nature finds. These can include pieces of driftwood, dried weeds, or bits of rocks and pebbles. On the wall behind this display mount grasses or dried weeds on construction paper (white glue that dries clear works well for this) to tie the whole theme together.

Urge students to develop their collections in categories. A sturdy shoe-box lid and cardboard "dividers" will make a collection box for items from a field trip or family outing. Cut the dividers to fit the box lid, glue the edges, and pin in place from the back. When these are dry, fill the sections with materials. A small scene can be placed in one section to tie the whole thing together. Glue ribbon around the box lid and hang. Be sure to glue down anything that might shift.

Dioramas. Dioramas are an attractive and concise way to share favorite books. Miniatures are very much in vogue, and students enjoy collecting all sorts of things to add to their small scenes of "life" from books.

Shoe boxes or candy boxes are good containers to use. When the student has planned the scene, the background is painted on the back panel and two sides of the box. This

scene should, of course, be appropriate to the setting of the
story. It can be a landscape including the sky and the "dis-
tant hills" or a forest or the far side of a building. If the
story has an outdoor setting, the "ground" can be made with
sand and rocks glued on modeling clay that has been molded
to the desired shape. Twigs and bits of sponge make good
trees. Figures can be built from modeling clay or shaped
from telephone cable wire. Wire figures should be covered
fur or cloth material.

    Plan to set dioramas at eye level on shelves for view-
ing.

MURALS

    One sixth-grade classroom in a Midwest elementary
school was visited by every other class in the school for the
purpose of viewing an eighteen-foot-long mural illustrated by
the entire class and entitled "Nothing Ever Happens in My
School!" Figures on the mural were involved in every con-
ceivable type of activity, ranging from the care of an injured
youngster on the playground to the annual visit by members
of the fire department. Members of this class were heard to
boast that the mural showed 262 separate activities that can
and often do take place during a single school day! The development of the mural came from a sharing of Ellen Raskin's
Nothing Ever Happens on My Block (Atheneum, 1974; see first
edition of E IS FOR EVERYBODY, page 60), a little gem of
a book that points up how unaware we can be of the myriad
activities that constantly occur around us. Aside from the
obvious enjoyment of sharing their artistic project with students from other classes, these sixth-graders were helped
through this project to become AWARE! Before the mural

Felt-on-burlap banner made by second-graders (photo courtesy of Lindberg School District, St. Louis County, Mo.)

was completed, committees from the class had interviewed
school employees, from principal to custodian, to gain a
clearer picture of each person's job.   Students were able to
see their own roles and responsibilities more clearly as they
examined their roles in relationship to the roles of others.
This increased awareness of the contributions of administra-
tors, teachers, noninstructional staff, students, and parents
to the total educational process helped students to accept more
responsibility for their own actions.

        If a particular work of literature holds great appeal
for an entire class, what better way can there be for students
to work together to change or add to the elements of the story
to create their own artistic work than through a mural!   In
constructing a mural, every child in the class is allowed to
contribute, and no contribution is too small, for all are necessary to create a unified whole in which the entire class
can take pride.   Almost any fine children's book can serve
as the basis for a class mural.

        Constructing a Mural.   In constructing a mural, the
                                basic guideline to follow is
THE BIGGER THE BETTER!   If possible, one entire side of
the classroom or a long portion of the hall outside the classroom should be used for the mural.   Figures drawn should be
very large.   (If human figures are required, students can use
large poster roll paper and draw around themselves.)   Large
figures can then be decorated with scraps of construction paper
and outlined with black felt-tip markers.   Some lines within
each figure may also need to be outlined, as well as the outer
edges of the figure.   As figures are cut out, they can be
mounted on the wall with masking tape rolled into loops.

        Another quite attractive mural can be done on large
roll paper by painting outlines of major figures or objects

with large brushes in black and completing the shapes or figures with color.   Brushes for outlining should be at least $\frac{1}{2}$" in width.   Smaller brushes can be used for filling in the color.

3.

BOOK-MAKING

Judith Viorst has written a classic tale that is a delight
to every elementary student: Alexander and the Terrible,
Horrible, No Good, Very Bad Day (Atheneum, 1974; see
first edition of E IS FOR EVERYBODY, page 74). After both
laughing and sympathizing over the plight of Alexander (for
who has not at one time or another had a terrible, horrible
day?), a fourth-grade class decided to write a sequel to the
book. Young hands went eagerly to their dictionaries to find
as many words as possible that meant GOOD. The title for
the sequel as finally devised was very likely the longest title
ever given a book! Following a class discussion during which
children had an opportunity to suggest something good that
could happen to Alexander, each student began work on an illustrated page for a book that the class would together write
and assemble. Each page would show one child's idea of
"Alexander's Very Best Day." The work was painstakingly
done. Texts were written and rewritten with care toward
spelling and punctuation before being placed on the final page
to be included in the book. Completed pages were laminated,
a cover designed, a title-and-author page developed. The
book was "bound" with metal rings and placed on the RARE
BOOK shelf in the school library for others to enjoy. What
pride these young authors had in the final product!

    Themes for class books can be found in humorous
stories like "Alexander" or can come from more serious
works like Kennedy's The Lost Kingdom of Karnica (entry 58),
which deals with the destruction of the environment. But
whatever book sparks young imaginations to creative writing
and illustrating, great benefits will be derived when a class
works together to develop its own book to be enjoyed by others
for years to come.

    Consistency is the most important element to consider
in making a class book. Be consistent with the paper used

by students for their final work.   Use the same size and quality paper for each student.   Any drawings or paintings should be done on the same kind of paper, using the same medium. The medium selected should not wrinkle or crack with handling. Felt-tip markers, watercolors, or crayons are most successful for this use.   Students do the initial illustrations with pencil and, when satisfied with the results, go over them with felt-tip markers or crayons.

Binding the Book.   For the cover and spine of the book the following materials are needed:

1) poster board that is at least six-ply (twelve-ply is better);

2) bookbinding tape at least 1" in width;

3) brass paper fasteners;

4) gummed reinforcements for each page (front and back);

5) a ruler.

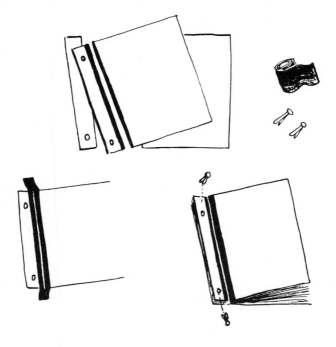

Measure the size of the pages. Cut two pieces of
poster board $\frac{1}{4}$" narrower and 1" longer than the size of the
pages. These are the back and front covers of the book.
Also cut two strips of poster board 1" wider and 1" longer
than the size of the pages. Tape one of these long narrow
strips to each of the covers with one long piece of bookbinding
tape. It will be stronger if taped on both sides. Punch all
the pages of the book. Lay the pages on the covers and mark
the holes on the narrow strips. Punch holes and insert brass
fasteners through all.

The cover can be designed in various ways. Don't forget the title. If cut-paper letters are used, glue them to the
cover and coat with polymer or clear contact paper. If anything is glued to the cover, it is better to use thin white glue
painted on the surface rather than spots of glue. Remember
that the book will receive considerable handling and should be
securely done.

Success can also be obtained by laminating individual
pages and fastening them together with rings. A cover can
be made from construction paper, which can also be laminated.

Stitching bindings is a tedious process and is not recom-
mended for elementary students.

4.

PUPPETS AND PAPIER-MÂCHÉ FIGURES

PUPPETS

The use of puppets in the classroom can turn shy little girls into haughty queens or boisterous little boys into quiet elves. Wonderful things do happen when children create their own puppets and develop the scripts for puppet plays based on favorite stories. James Thurber's Many Moons (Harcourt Brace Jovanovich, 1973, originally published in 1943) makes a perfect vehicle for a puppet play in which the entire class can become involved. Rather than a single puppet stage, impromptu puppet stages can appear all over the room as card tables are turned on their sides for use by young puppeteers. The roaring king, the spoiled princess, the court jester, and all of the children of the kingdom provide parts for every

member of the class.   Books mentioned in E IS FOR EVERY-
BODY that can become delightful puppet plays are Gammell's
Once Upon MacDonald's Farm (entry 38), John Goodall's
Paddy's New Hat (entry 42), Kalen's Jump, Frog, Jump (entry
55), Kennedy's Lost Kingdom of Karnica (entry 58), and
Moeri's The Unicorn and the Plow (entry 76).   In fact, any
book that has great appeal to the children of a particular
class can be transformed into a puppet play.

   The photographs on page 155 and page 158 show, first,
a couple of hand puppets more ambitious than those for which
directions are given here--but someone talented with needle
and thread can often be encouraged to pitch in!--and a couple
of finger puppets made from dried vegetables.

   Puppets have greatest appeal when they have the following characteristics:

   1) The puppet must move.

   2) The puppeteer must not be obvious.   His or her efforts
      to move the puppet must be well hidden.

   3) If the puppet speaks, it must be heard by the audience.

   4) The puppet must be sturdy enough to hold up under all
      acting conditions.

   Puppets that meet these requirements and that can be
made by elementary students include stick puppets, paper-bag
puppets, sock puppets, paper-plate puppets, hand puppets,
and papier-mâché puppets.   Directions for making each of
these follow.

   Stick Puppets.   Draw a figure, cut it out, and mount
                    it on tag board; cut it out again and
fasten a stick to the back.   Bend the arms and legs so they
will "jiggle" when the figure is moved.   Remember, the more
it moves the more interest it creates.   (See Figure A.)

   Paper-Bag Puppets.   A paper bag makes an excellent
                        puppet.   Stuff the head and tie at
the neck.   Add features that flop, accordion-pleated arms, etc.,
and insert a stick to hold it.   (See Figure B.)

   Sock Puppets.   See the steps illustrated on page 159
                   for the construction of a sock puppet.

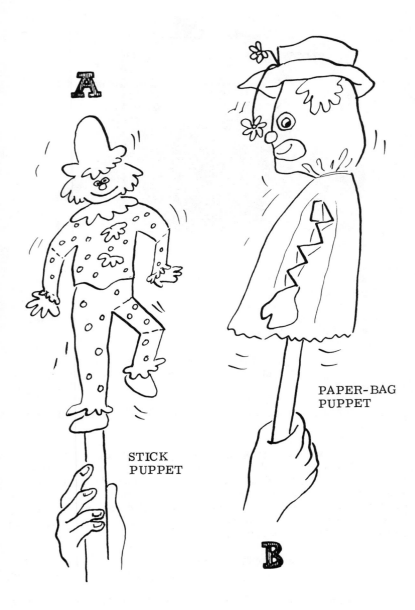

STICK
PUPPET

PAPER-BAG
PUPPET

1) Slit the toe of a large sock--this will become the puppet's mouth.

2) Insert an oval of material; in order for it to hold well,
   it should be stitched in.

3) The child's (or teacher's!) four fingers are put into
   the upper part of the mouth and the thumb into the
   lower part.

4) Stitch on buttons for eyes, yarn hair, and felt or cloth
   ears.

      Make features prominent with size, color, and place-
ment.   You might want to stuff some features to bring them
out.   Make a puppet yourself, along with your students, to
read poems and stories for your class.   Watch Sesame Street
or some other puppet show with your own creations in mind.
Discuss them with your students.   Talk about some things you
can do to enhance your creations.

      Paper-Plate Puppets.   See the steps illustrated below
                            for making a paper-plate puppet.

1) A paper plate folded in half becomes the puppet's mouth.

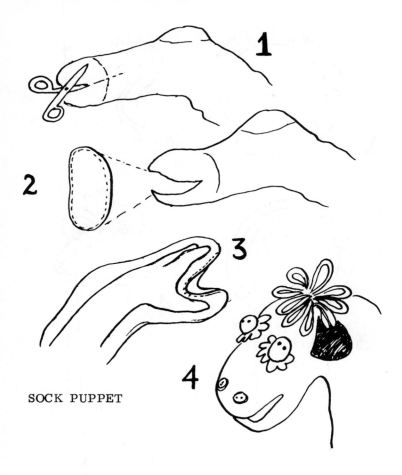

SOCK PUPPET

2) Opening and closing the hand makes the puppet seem to talk.

3) An old pajama leg becomes an effective arm- and hand-hider; glue the open end of the leg to the back of the plate.

4) Give the puppet construction-paper eyes--glue them to the top of the folded plate so they will stand up.

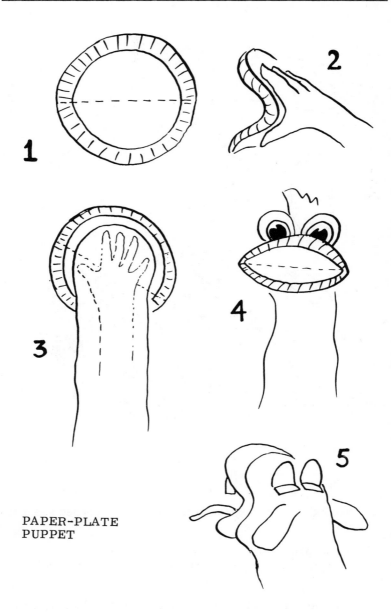

PAPER-PLATE
PUPPET

5) Construction-paper tongue and teeth can be put in the
critter's mouth.   Yarn can become hair, and stuffed
stockings can be long floppy ears!

Hand Puppets--A Variation.   Simple hand puppets in
                             which the puppeteer can
make the arms, head, and body of the puppet move are illustrated A, B, and C on page 162.   For A a styrofoam ball
becomes the puppet's head.   Push a dowel rod in the bottom
of the ball to make a place for your finger to go in.   Push
in the top front of the ball on the edge of a table to make
the face (look carefully at illustration A); the forehead may
be slightly flattened as well.   Decorate with felt features.
Add a "dress"--as explained next.

For the "Lion" (illustration B) a toe of a sock, stuffed
and with a cardboard tube glued in the bottom makes a good
head.   Glue on felt features.   Add "dress."   For C a piece
of old sheeting cut and sewn as shown makes a simple hand
puppet.   Stuff the head with a little cotton and use magic
markers for the features.

Basic Puppet "Dress."   To give the appearance of
                        clothes and a body to the A
or B kind of simple hand puppets, make a dress for them
(see illustration).   Draw around the student's hand with the
fingers extended as shown.   Leave a stitching margin and
redraw the dress to fit the hand.   Leave an opening at the
"neck."   Stitch both sides.   Fit the dress onto or into the
puppet's head and glue in place.   Decorate with felt, buttons,
ribbon, etc.

Puppet Stage.   Here are a couple of simple stages for
                your classroom (see illustrations on
page 164).   First, an open doorway makes an excellent stage:
hand the upper scenery (painted or drawn on cloth or paper)
from the hall side of the top of the doorway.   Hang the lower
part (which hides the puppeteer and provides the stage) across
the bottom third or so of the doorway, on the classroom side.
The puppeteers kneel just outside the doorway and operate
their puppets against the upper backdrop.

At the bottom of page 164 is shown a stage made from
a large cardboard box, not too deep, with the bottom cut out,
which is turned on its side and placed on the back edge of a
small table.   Hang a curtain over the table to hide the puppeteers and also hang a curtain over the open back of the box.
Add wings (as illustrated) if there are several actors to hide.

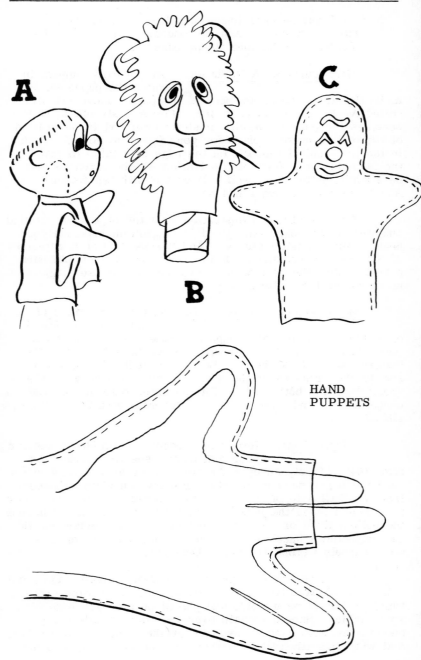

A

B

C

HAND
PUPPETS

PAPIER-MÂCHÉ FIGURES

Author William Armstrong paid a visit to a public library where an autograph party was being held in his honor. Excited children knowing well in advance about the visit of this beloved author of <u>Sounder</u> (Harper & Row, 1969) prepared for their meeting with him by constructing a life-sized papier-mâché figure of Sounder. The careful research that went into finding every possible characteristic of this noble hunting dog and the painstaking detail incorporated in the development of the figure were obvious to all who saw and admired it. The only thing more obvious on that memorable afternoon was the pride of the young artists!

Making papier-mâché figures has long been a favorite art activity of boys and girls. How delightful it is to be a part of a classroom that is filled with beloved characters from books! The construction of such figures cannot be done in one work period. Drying time must be allowed between layers of paper applied to a figure and between coats of paint. A good period of time to plan on in one daily work period on the figures for about one week. "Mess" can be minimized with the following suggestions:

1) Use wallpaper paste rather than flour and water.

2) Mix in a large bucket beginning with water and slowly adding paste until it is the consistency of cream. Stir as paste is added. It will thicken past the cream stage but will remain at the workable stage.

3) Cover all work areas with newspaper. Students should tear working strips before receiving paste.

4) Use nonbreakable, throwaway containers, such as butter tubs, plastic ice cream containers, or gallon milk jugs with the top cut off for individual paste.

5) Have plenty of waste containers available for cleanup.

6) Do not empty paste down sinks. Scrape out paste containers into newspapers. Large amounts of paste can be covered and kept one day beyond preparation.

7) For drying the figures have a place ready that is large enough to accommodate them.

8) Use wet sponges for cleanup.

(cut-away view)

SHOW

PERRONIQUE

PUPPET STAGES

In building a papier-mâché figure, one must begin with a basic form. The form can be constructed from rolled-up newspapers (as in the construction of an animal), or, if the figure will be very fat, a balloon can be used. Once the form is completed, strips of paper are dipped in the wallpaper paste and molded to the form as shown in the illustrations that follow.

Balloons take two people: one must hold while another puts on strips. Six to eight layers are best. Allow to dry thoroughly before adding features.

When all layers of papier-mâché are dry, prick balloon and remove it. Fill with candy or "prizes" if desired. Decorate figure with crepe-paper and construction-paper features.

A long thin balloon makes a long thin critter. For jaws
add rolled newspaper folded in half and flattened.   (See next
illustration.)   Feet are made of cardboard.

Roll up two sheets of newspaper the long way and tape with
masking tape for each body part.   Tape the rolls together to
form body (many kinds of figures can be made--the above is
just an example).   Cover bodies with four to six layers of
newspaper strips soaked in wallpaper paste.

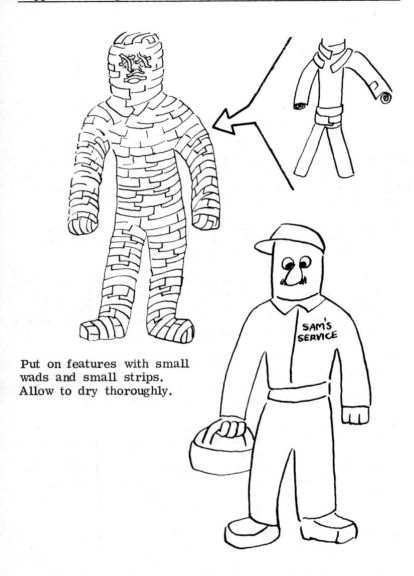

Put on features with small
wads and small strips.
Allow to dry thoroughly.

SAM'S
SERVICE

Paint facial features and hands with tempera.   Try doll
clothes, hats, and accessories, or paint some and make
others from construction paper or cardboard.   Coat painted
surfaces with polymer to keep paint from flaking, or spray
with hair spray.

5

SLIDES AND FILMSTRIPS

In Reading Guidance in a Media Age (Polette and Hamlin, Scarecrow Press, 1975) the following values are noted. In producing a sound filmstrip or sound/slide show based on a work of literature, the student will:

1) Demonstrate ability to comprehend, interpret, and communicate to others the author's ideas and express them in the written or spoken word.

2) Show understanding and appreciation of the basic elements of literature. Plot, setting, characterization, theme, and style all take on a clarity and meaning when the student attempts to communicate these elements to others through an audiovisual presentation.

3) Demonstrate ability to clarify an idea or concept and to present it in symbolic form. (The small amount of space available to work on a filmstrip or slide forces the student to illustrate an idea symbolically.)

4) Select main concepts, ideas, or events relevant to the story. When a work of literature is too long for a complete student production, the student selects those parts of the story that will keep the plot running smoothly and that will best interpret the story to others. The theme must be identified, and portions of the story that best support the theme are emphasized.

5) Gain expertise in organization and in developing ideas in logical sequence. The preparation of the storyboard (text with proposed visuals) forces the student to think logically and to communicate ideas in well-developed, sequential steps.

6) Extend thought processes through the process of substi-

tuting one visual for another to express the same idea.
Long after a slide show is completed, a student will
find a visual he or she feels is better to use in express-
ing an idea. It is rare that a show is ever considered
so perfect that it cannot be improved, and students often
strive to do this.

7) Have an opportunity to find his or her "place in the
sun." Slide and filmstrip production is not difficult.
Using these techniques, every student can use creativity
to the fullest.

The processes for producing filmstrips and slides are
relatively inexpensive and require no special talent on the
part of the student other than the ability to present a story
in logical, sequential form.

CONTACT SLIDES

Materials Needed:

transparent contact paper cut into 2"x2" squares;

slide mounts;

glossy magazine pictures or catalog pictures;

shallow pan (for soaking the slides);

bar of handsoap;

iron (for mounting if cardboard slide mounts are used);

old cloth (for wiping slides off);

tongue depressors--several (optional).

Steps to Follow:

1) Find a magazine picture, size 2"x2". Children can use
a "finder" constructed by cutting a hole 2"x2" from a
sheet of paper or cardboard; this may be used when
scanning magazines to discover whether a certain picture fits into a slide of this size.

2) Peel the protective wax paper from the 2"x2" square
of contact paper you have cut in advance. Lay the exposed adhesive side on the picture starting from one
end and working toward the other.

3) Press over the contact paper, applying as much pres-
sure as possible with a tongue depressor or a fisted
hand. This is to ensure that the adhesive and ink make
the best contact possible.

4) Soak this square in warm soapy water for several minutes. After awhile the paper will loosen from the contact paper and may be removed much like the backing
from a decal--slide it off. If the backing is stubborn,
use a dampened cloth to rub gently and crumble the paper
away. The contact paper remaining is now clearly im-
printed with the image. Allow this to dry.

5) Because the inked surface is still adhesive, place another 2"x2" contact piece over this to protect it.

6) Now you are ready to mount the transparency. You
may use the size 127 cardboard super-slide mounts,
which require the contact piece to be sandwiched between
the layers and pressed with a hot iron around the edges
(kids love pressing these), or you may use 35mm plastic mounts, which require no pressing, just cropping the
picture to a smaller size and sliding it into a built-in
holder.

7) Your slide is now ready for projection. Slides are pro-
jected on any standard slide projector or through use of
a filmstrip projector with slide attachment.

Variations for this project include trapping pieces of
colored tissue paper between the sheets of contact paper for
original and stained-glass effects. Also, to create title slides
or drawn slides, cover the adhesive side of the contact square
with 3M Magic Tape or Scotch Mystic Tape and write or draw
with heavy markers onto the tape. For best results use the
2"-wide tape.

ADDITIONAL METHODS FOR MAKING SLIDES

1) Damaged commercial transparencies

a) Secure permission from producer to use portions of damaged commercial transparencies for slides.

b) Place 2"x2" slide frame over those portions of the transparency that would adapt well to slide use.

c) Outline the area on the transparency to be used with grease pencil or visual-aid pen.

d) Cut and mount slide.

e) The slide is now ready to project.

2) Xerox/transparency slides

a) Obtain publisher's permission to make a xerox copy of illustrations from a book.

b) Select illustrations, in black-and-white only, that have small figures.

c) Make a xerox copy of the illustration(s).

d) Cut from the xerox copy 2"x2" squares, using those portions of the illustrations that demonstrate the main points of the story, article, etc.

e) Glue illustrations in sequential order on an $8\frac{1}{2}$"x11" sheet of white paper (each sheet should hold twenty-four 2"x2" pictures).

f) Make a transparency of the $8\frac{1}{2}$"x11" sheet with its glued illustrations.

g) Cut transparency into 2"x2" squares (one square for each illustration).

h) Mount transparency slides in slide frames.

i) If desired, slides may be colored, using 3M transparency-marking pens or Carter's visual-aid pens.

j) The slide is now ready to project.

3) Original slides

a) Select a story, article, problem, etc., to be illustrated.

b) Read carefully and mark off in segments to be illustrated. (Note: one slide is usually needed for each four to six lines of text.)

c) Rule off (with pencil) an $8\frac{1}{2}$"x11" sheet of plain white paper into 2"x2" squares.

d) Write the title in square 1, author in square 2, illustrator in square 3.

e) Using a pencil, draw in sequence the illustrations to accompany the story. Use fairly heavy pencil lines.

f) Make a transparency of the $8\frac{1}{2}$"x11" sheet with its completed drawing.

g) Cut sheet apart into its previously ruled 2"x2" squares.

h) Mount transparency slides in slide frames.

i) If desired, slides may be colored, using 3M transparency-marking pens or Carter's visual-aid pens.

j) The slide is now ready to project.

WRITE-ON FILMSTRIPS

U film, or 35mm clear film, is blank film divided into frames and with appropriate sprocket holes to fit any standard filmstrip projector. It can usually be obtained at photo-supply stores. Students prepare the script and plan each frame to accompany the narration. Illustrations can be planned on plain white paper using squares the size of a U film frame. Illustrations are placed on U film or 35mm clear film using felt-tip markers, pen, pencil, colored pencils, or typewriter. The outline of the illustration should be kept between the two black dots on the film and should be as simple as possible.

SUBJECT INDEX TO PART I

[Numbers refer to entries, not pages.]

ABC books 48, 52, 63, 65, 124
acrostic poetry 44
advice 18
Africa 1, 7, 53
aircraft 93
Alaska 40
Alice in Wonderland 6
alliteration 110
American history 88, 92
animals 94, 101, 121
   African 1, 7, 53
   desert 91, 100
   fables 67, 87, 97
   forest 30, 55
   homes 8, 55, 98
   legendary 70
   paper 7
   sounds 63
antonyms 69
apartments 37
Arctic 52
art 112
associative thinking 27

babies 3
baboons 38
bakers 27
ballerinas 24, 33
balloons, hot-air 19, 113
battles 24
bears 34, 40, 52, 101
Beatles 6

bedspreads 36
beetles 21
Big Ben 6
birds 103
boa constrictors 78
bookmarks 69
books 18
booksellers 11
bravery 26
brothers 96
bulletin boards 7, 9, 19, 26, 30, 31, 37, 42, 110

camouflage 7
candy 11
cars 85
caterpillars 71
cats 19, 50, 51, 56, 59, 69, 84
   paper 51
cause and effect 23
chain-of-event stories 39, 55, 78
chameleons 7
childhood fears 26
choices 99, 119
Christ Child 114
Christmas 28, 114
churches 28
cinquains 45
circus wagons 39
circuses 28, 39, 74, 80

173